THE VEGAN REMIX!

A Soulful Spin On World Cuisine

BY AFYA IBOMU

Holistic Nutritionist, BS, CHHC

Author of *The Vegan Soul Food Guide To The Galaxy*

The Vegan Remix: A Soulful Spin on World Cuisine
Gluten Free and Allergy Friendly

ISBN-10:0-9831437-1-4
ISBN-13:978-0-9831437-1-0
Library of Congress Control Number: 2014922124

Food Photography: Afya Ibomu
Cover and Album Photography: Terra Coles
Interior and Cover Design: Shannon Washington
Editing: Carolyn Sanders and Details Count, Sis Abena Muhammed, Khnum Ibomu

Note to the reader: This book is to be considered as a reference work only, not a medical text. This material draws from the ancient systems as well as the author's own experience. The information contained in the following pages is in no way to be considered as a substitute for consultation, diagnosis or treatment by a duly licensed physician or other health care professional. This information is intended solely for use as a source of general information and not for application to any individual case. It is sold with the understanding that the publisher is not engaged in rendering medical advice. If you have a medical problem we urge you to seek a competent Holistic, Naturopathic or Medical health practitioner.

Published by:
Nattral Unlimited, LLC
PO Box 310330 Atlanta, Ga 31131
www.NATTRAL.com

www.nattral.com

nattral™
health culture style
www.nattral.com

TURN TABLE OF CONTENTS

STIR IT UP: SOUPS AND STEWS

OPENING ACTS: WRAPS AND SNACKS

SWEET NOTES: DESSERTS

POUR UP...DRANK: BEVERAGES

SAUCE IT UP: TASTY TOUCHES

ABOUT THE AUTHOR

INDEX

ACKNOWLEGEMENTS

I'd like to thank my family for always supporting me in my projects and life. I love you all and appreciate your unconditional encouragement.

Khnum, thanks for all of the time and energy you gave to this book. I couldn't have done it without your creative, marketing and writing expertise.

Give thanks Itwela for your patience when I was working and focusing on making this happen! You know what we are grinding for!

Mom, your support and love is always appreciated and thanks for helping out with whatever I need!

Shannon! This is the fourth book we've done together! Thanks for sticking in there with me to get it to the people! Love you girl!

"When you arise in the morning give thanks for the food and for the joy of living."
-Native American saying

- afya

FOREWORD

I've been vegetarian since 1989. When I moved to Brooklyn, New York, in 1997, I was introduced to the vegan lifestyle. Raising my children on vegan and vegetarian diets has had its challenges because each of them has different types of bodies and tolerances. The struggle was real with their food allergies, but you learn a little bit more as you go.

It can be frustrating sometimes for Vegan families, especially since seems like the general consensus is that we're making our children suffer if they're Vegan or Vegetarian just because the rest of the world really hasn't caught on. We sure don't want our children to feel like their diet is a punishment. What I'm concerned about the most is that my children know how to heal themselves with natural healing tools like water, greens and herbs.

Back in the 90's the whole vegan/vegetarian thing was new on the scene and we didn't have a lot of choices. We had to figure things out for ourselves or try to find an elder who was versed in this world of vegetarianism. Thankfully, I had the pleasure of meeting Afya. She traveled on tour and shared her nutritional wisdom with me, my children and tour mates. Afya was very helpful, I remember her making an herb bath for my son to help sooth his skin after a very intense allergic reaction.

Afya and I have been good friends for over 15 years now. I was there during her home birth with her son and that whole experience inspired me on my path as a Doula (birth assistant). Afya is my hero. She doesn't force her vegan diet on people, she is a Holistic nutritionist and shares my sentiment that you have to eat what's right for you. That's why I think this book is right on target, in so many ways.

Like music, foods can be a big part of our healing. Everything has a frequency and vibrates at a certain rate. I think it's all connected in a certain way, in a deep kind of way. The art of making music and making food is all about the chef and the composer's images that will take on the flavor that you add to the food. The food is a reflection of one's taste and is a unique combination of spices and herbs that you blend like a DJ.

For those that may suffer from food allergies, or just want to add more flavor and variety to your healthy meals, my girl got you covered! Afya has cooked up something special with *The Vegan Remix* and it will help bring healthier beings together on the planet!

Stay Woke,
E. Badu

PRESS PLAY ▶

The Vegan Remix has been a few years in the making. At first my vision was to just veganize some of my favorite recipes from my childhood and young adult life, giving them my own unique culinary spin. Then, a couple of years ago my husband and I found out that our son, Itwela, had food allergies. He is allergic to soy, gluten, and berries. This dramatically changed our diet and lifestyles. We are such a family of foodies and with this news we were no longer able to eat at most of our favorite restaurants. This included even the more vegan friendly places because they were either largely soy or gluten based or both. We also discovered that most restaurants cook with soybean based vegetable oil.

I had to adapt to cooking at home more often with allergy friendly options in mind. I had to educate myself on new ingredients, how they worked together, what could be used as substitutions, and so much more. There were all kinds of new flours, new grains, and new types of protein to try. I couldn't just sauté a block of tofu or some seitan as I had been doing for years. I needed time to experiment and get used to this new way of cooking. I worked on many new recipes but they just were not coming out right.

After a few years of cooking, researching, and experimenting, I started to find my groove. I would turn on and turn up my favorite music playlist and jam out while I worked on the recipes. Hip Hop and music in general is always a big part of my lifestyle. Just as Hip Hop producers create their magic in the studio by sampling and making hot new creations, I approach cooking with that same creative vibe.

Since food and music are such a large influence in my life, the Vegan Remix seemed to be one of the best ways to express these recipes. This book is a mix of recipes that are inspired by foods that I ate while growing up, some of my favorite dishes from restaurants, and a few things I've just come up with over the years with a focus on allergy friendly options. When my son was diagnosed with allergies, my eyes were also opened to the growing number of people with food allergies. Whether you are allergic to soy, gluten, dairy, nuts, or

anything else, it can be difficult to find tasty foods to eat, especially if you are vegan or plant based.

There are over ninety plant based, allergy friendly recipes in this book to show that just because you have food allergies it doesn't mean you can't enjoy good tasty food! Each recipe is noted to determine which allergens are included or not. There are soy free, gluten free, dairy free, nut free and grain free options available. I have used specific brands in this book, which I usually don't do because it may not be possible to find all foods in every city. Also, companies and brands change over time with the quality and taste of their products possibly changing and some products discontinuing. But, practically speaking, some recipes are just easier to make and taste better with certain brands. Please feel free to use some of your favorite brands as well. I've also included music playlists in the book that served as my soundtrack while cooking and creating! I love a range of music so hopefully you will be inspired to mix up some good vibes while you are cooking too!

I am overjoyed to present this collection of selections that have rocked at our house and hopefully they will rock your world as well... Whatever your allergy or food choice there is something in this book for you.

Have Fun. Enjoy. Turn Up and Rock Out!
- afya

HOW TO USE THIS BOOK

Each recipe indicates which allergens have been omitted from them. The index has sections organized by which allergies are omitted in specific recipes and types of cuisines. Also, you will find full color pages throughout the book to get a detailed, up close look at finished recipes.

THE WARM UP

WHEAT, GLUTEN AND OTHER GRAINS

Grains are a type of carbohydrate that serves as a source of energy in your body. Whole grains are high in B vitamins, fiber, and protein. Choosing whole grains instead of processed white grains can help you to lose weight, eat less, control your cravings, lower your insulin, give you more energy and help you to be more focused. When whole grains (complex carbohydrates) are eaten, they break down into complex sugars, unlike white rice that converts into simple sugars. Whole grain complex carbohydrates digest at a much slower rate than simple ones. This slowed down process allows your blood sugar, as well as your energy, to remain stable and consistent throughout the day. Unfortunately some people are allergic to certain grains whether they are whole or not. The most popular grain allergy is to gluten. Celiac disease is one of the most common diagnoses of gluten intolerance but just because you are allergic to gluten does not necessarily mean you have celiac disease. Luckily, there are a whole host of grains that are gluten free and easy to find.

WHAT IS GLUTEN?

Gluten is a protein present in wheat and other whole grains such as barley, rye, spelt, kamut, and some oats. Gluten helps dough to rise and lends shape and a chewy texture to baked goods.

GLUTEN FREE WHOLE GRAINS

Rice (brown, black, red) is the most widely consumed staple food for most of the world's human population. Different types of rice have become more popular in the United States such as black and

The Best Way to Prepare Whole Grains And Legumes

Soaking and sprouting are the best ways to prepare whole grains and legumes (beans). Some people are not able to eat grains and legumes due to intestinal issues but over time can eat small amounts of sprouts. Sprouting is a way to soak beans, grains and seeds to enhance their enzymes, vitamins, minerals and digestibility. The grain or seeds opens up (germinates) and helps breaks down anti-nutrient factors like phytic acid. Soaking grains in baking soda for a minimum of five minutes also helps to remove phytic acids and reduce cooking times.

red. These types are more nutritious than brown or white rice and just as tasty.

Wild rice is indigenous to North America and was heavily used by the Ojibwa and Sioux people. It is thought to be over 12,000 years old. Wild rice is a great source of protein and zinc.

Quinoa (pronounced keen-wah) has been used for 6,000 years by the Incan people in South America. It's a complete protein and also contains, folate, zinc and calcium. There is a debate about whether quinoa is a seed or a grain. It is technically a seed but due to its high carbohydrate content, it's labeled a pseudo-cereal, making it neither cereal nor grain. As a matter of fact, it is more closely related to spinach and beets. Some people who may be sensitive to grains may also be sensitive to quinoa. Buckwheat is also in this pseudo-cereal category.

Corn is thought of by many people as a vegetable but it is actually a grain. It was cultivated thousands of years ago in Mesoamerica and was one of the staple grains of indigenous American people. These days it's important to only eat and purchase organic corn due to the Genetic Modification of nearly all non-organic corn.

Millet is a grain that's indigenous to Africa. It's high in protein and is similar to couscous in texture.

Teff is a delicious grain from Ethiopia and is one of the oldest grains in the world. It is high in protein and most commonly used in a spongy bread recipe called injera.

Amaranth has been cultivated as a grain for 8,000 years and was a staple food of the Aztec people in ancient America.

Oats are naturally gluten free but they may be contaminated with gluten. Most commercial oats are processed in facilities that also process wheat, barley, and rye. Also contamination can happen in the field, when oats are grown side-by-side with wheat or other gluten containing grains. So its best to only purchase oats labeled gluten free.

Gluten-Free Flour Options

FLOURS / STARCHES	NUT FLOURS
Arrowroot flour	Almond flour
Cornstarch	Chestnut flour
Potato flour	Coconut flour
Potato starch	Hazelnut flour
Sorghum flour	
Rice flour	BEAN FLOURS
Tapioca flour	Fava bean flour
Corn meal	Garbanzo bean flour
Teff	
All-purpose mix	Gram flour

NON-WHOLE GRAINS

Foods *made* with whole grains are not the same thing as an actual whole grain. These are processed foods made from whole grains. They *are* healthier for you than white flour products because they have more nutrients, but they are still processed and if eaten in excess, even processed foods made with whole grains can cause weight gain and other health issues. Examples are whole grain cereal, flour, and various whole grain baked goods.

Flour is a powder made from ground up grains, corn, seeds, or beans. Wheat flour is one of the most popular flours used in the U.S. but since so many people are being diagnosed as allergic or sensitive to gluten, many other gluten free flour options are becoming more popular.

All-purpose gluten free flour can be purchased as a pre-mix of many different types of gluten free ingredients. They can be a mix of garbanzo bean flour, potato starch, tapioca flour, sorghum flour, rice flour and fava bean flour. This really helps to ease the baking process because you don't have to find all the ingredients yourself and the mixture also helps to achieve the texture and consistency desired for gluten free baking.

GLUTEN-FREE PASTA

There are many different varieties of allergy friendly versions of pasta. Rice, quinoa, corn and cous cous pastas can be found in most grocery stores around the country, including the grocery sections of Target and Wal-Mart. Make sure you read the cooking directions because some gluten free pastas only take a few minutes to cook. I always cook these pastas for less time than the package says because gluten free options can become mushy very easily. After draining, immediately run the pasta under cold water to stop the cooking process.

TOFU, BEANS AND OTHER PROTEINS

It can seem challenging to get enough protein when you are vegan and allergic to soy. Luckily, there

are a variety of other beans as well as nuts and seeds to get protein from. But let's dig in a little deeper and see what's up with all the soy controversy anyway.

THE QUESTION OF SOY

There is a lot of controversy about the safety of eating soy. In my understanding, the main concern is in which type of soy we eat, the amounts we consume, and what process it goes through. Soy, along with other legumes (beans), contains chemicals called trypsin inhibitors and phytates. These chemicals can cause digestive issues and even a decrease in nutrients in the body. Soaking, fermenting and sprouting soy and beans helps to decrease these inhibitors to allow your body to digest them safely. Also, most non-organic soybeans are genetically modified and heavily sprayed with pesticides. So eating organic soy is the best option.

Top 8 Allergens List	
Milk	Soy
Eggs	Fish
Wheat	Tree nuts
Peanuts	Shellfish

The soy industry is expanding and now various, highly processed soy derivatives are showing up in cereals, energy bars, breads, soups and gravies in forms such as soy oil, soy protein isolate and hydrolyzed vegetable protein. Over-processed food, whether vegan or not, is not a whole food and is a foreign substance to your body. Over-consumption of these types of over processed soy products can contribute to cancer, thyroid problems, weight gain, bloating, excess mucus, and food allergies. I know these foods are quick, easy, and tasty, but please be aware of how much you are consuming. Eating these foods for breakfast, lunch and dinner is too much. Mix up your protein sources with other beans, quinoa, and veggies.

Soy, even if it isn't highly processed, is also one of the top eight allergens in the U.S. Some people are born allergic to the protein in soy and some develop an allergy to it because of eating too much of it, or eating a lot of overly processed soy. Organic tempeh, miso, sprouted tofu and gluten free low sodium soy sauce are the best choices for soy consumption. But eat them moderately, not excessively, no more than three to four times per week.

Tofu (toe-foo) is made from soybeans. The beans are boiled, ground up and solidified. It can be made or bought in a variety of different textures and consistencies based off of the amount of water added

CUTTING TOFU

The five different ways to cut tofu.

SLICED

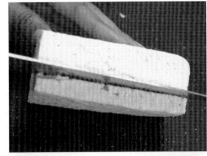

STEAKS

STRIPS

NUGGETS

CUBES

to it. It comes in silken, soft, firm, and extra firm. Silken and soft are best used for blended ingredients, cakes, pies, and puddings. Firm and extra firm are good for slicing, baking, sautéing, and grilling. I've discovered that tofu is much more flavorful if it is marinated first for at least 30 minutes to overnight before you cook with it. I have been practicing as a vegan so long that I rarely marinate tofu and have found a few tricks to add flavor as I am cooking. Tofu can also be frozen and thawed to give it more of a meatier, firmer texture. Some people squeeze the water out of tofu before using it, but I usually don't unless I've frozen it first.

Sprouted Tofu is made from soybeans that have been soaked and sprouted. The sprouting helps to increase digestibility and reduce the phytates that can lead to health problems. It's higher in protein, fat and calcium than unsprouted tofu. It's still not an option for those allergic to soy but for others who aren't allergic to soy, it is a better choice than regular tofu. Sprouted soy may be hard to find in certain areas so call around or look on the Internet.

Tempeh (tem-pay) is made from fermented soybeans and one of the best forms of soy. It's high in protein and has a sweet nutty flavor. Tempeh can be fried, baked, sautéed or grilled. It has a very unique flavor and should always be marinated or well seasoned. There are many options for pre-seasoned tempeh that taste pretty good. I've also seen non-soy Tempeh made from black beans and black-eyed peas instead of soy. The non-soy forms of Tempeh can be difficult to find, so check around on the Internet.

Beans are one of the best sources of plant-based protein. There are numerous kinds and they are so versatile, they can be eaten almost every day. Some people have issues with gas when they eat beans because their system is not use to their high soluble fiber content, or because they have not been soaked or sprouted. Starting with easier to digest beans such as lentils and split peas, can allow your body to slowly adjust. Then in a few weeks you could add others like, chickpeas, butter beans, and pigeon peas. Red beans and black beans are two of the hardest beans to digest so add those into your diet last. Soaking beans in water and baking soda overnight, then skimming the bubbles of foam off the top of them while they are cooking, helps to get rid of some of the gas. Cooking them with kombu (kelp) helps reduce the gas as well. Dried beans can take up to an hour or more to cook, so keep canned or, better still, frozen beans on hand for a quick meal.

NUTS AND SEEDS

Nuts and seeds are high in protein and necessary fat. They can be eaten as snacks, in smoothies, on salads and even as a garnish. Nuts get a bad rap because they are high in fat, but they are high in the fats that our body needs. Even though nuts are healthy for most, they are also one of the top eight allergens. Some people are allergic to ground nuts like peanuts. Others may be allergic to tree nuts (walnut, pecans, almond, hazelnut, cashew, coconuts, pistachio, and brazil nuts).

Allergy-friendly Seeds

Seeds can be a great alternative option for those allergic to nuts. They are an easy way to add protein and omega fatty acids to your diet. There are seed butters and spreads that can be a great remix for things like peanut butter.

Flax Seeds

Flax seeds are high in fiber and omega-3 fatty acids. Studies have shown that flax seeds have laxative effects and may lower cholesterol levels. They may also benefit individuals with certain types of breast and prostate cancers and lessen the severity of diabetes by stabilizing blood-sugar levels. Flax seeds should be ground up before they are consumed raw because they cannot be chewed up well enough and can get caught in your digestive system and cause health issues.

Hemp Seeds

Hemp protein contains all 21 known amino acids, including the nine essential ones adult bodies cannot produce on their own. The amino acid profile of hemp seeds is close to "complete" when compared to more common sources of proteins such as meat, milk, eggs and soy. Hemp seeds are also a good source of zinc and omega fatty acids. Hemp seeds can contain trace amounts of THC, the component in marijuana that makes you high, but you have to consume such large amounts that it's really impossible to get high on hemp seeds. As far as drug tests are concerned, you would have to consume 1/2 cup of hemp oil or 40 tablespoons of hemp seeds a day for a significant amount of time to test positive. Many brands will label if their seeds contain THC or not.

Hemp Tofu

Hemp tofu is a healthy high protein alternative to soy-based tofu. It's free of allergens and easy to

digest. Hemp tofu has more of a texture like tempeh than tofu but it's not as bitter tasting as tempeh. Hemp tofu can be found in health food stores and there are also recipes on the internet for making it yourself at home.

Sesame Seeds

Sesame is one of the oldest cultivated plants in the world, prized as an oil seed for at least 5,000 years. Sesame seeds contain calcium, iron, folate, protein and magnesium. It's history as a medicine goes back 3,600 years to Egypt. Women in ancient Babylon were believed to use a mixture of honey and sesame seeds, called *havla*, to prolong youth and beauty. Roman soldiers ate the mixture for strength and energy. Sesame seeds and their oil have also been shown to be helpful in diseases such as diabetes, high blood pressure, and gingivitis.

Chia Seeds

Chia seeds are tiny, power-packed seeds that come from a desert plant grown in Mexico dating back to Mayan and Aztec cultures. "Chia" means strength, and these seeds are used as an energy booster. Chia seeds are a nutrient-dense food – one ounce (about 2 tablespoons) contains 4 grams of protein, 9 grams of fat, 179 mg of calcium, 2 mg of iron, 11 grams of fiber, and many healthy omega-3 fatty acids. Chia seeds are an unprocessed, whole-grain food that can be absorbed by the body as seeds (unlike flax seeds). The mild, nutty flavor of chia seeds makes them easy to add to foods and beverages. They are most often sprinkled on cereal, sauces, vegetables, rice dishes, yogurt or mixed into drinks and baked goods. They can also be mixed with water and made into a gel. Sometimes people complain that chia seeds may cause stomach upset. Chia seeds naturally absorb water and can absorb water in the digestive tract, which may lead to discomfort. I like to pre-soak my seeds in water before use. Here is a quick and simple way to do it:

Soaked Chia Seeds
1 tablespoon of chia seeds
3/4 cup water

Add chia seeds and water into a small glass container with a tight fitting top. Mix seeds around

so that they don't stick together or to the jar. Let sit for 30 minutes. Mix again, making sure nothing is sticking. Cover and store in the refrigerator for up to 2 weeks. Use chia mixture in smoothies, cereal, soups and more.

Pumpkin Seeds
Pumpkin seeds have long been valued as a source of the mineral zinc, and the World Health Organization recommends their consumption as a good way of obtaining this nutrient. A 1/2 cup of shelled roasted pumpkin seeds contains about 7 to 8 milligrams of zinc and 19 grams of protein. The seeds also contain vitamin E, iron, and calcium. They can be added to salads, smoothies and cereal.

Sunflower Seeds
Sunflower seeds are the gift of the beautiful sunflower that produces grayish-green or black seeds and have been used for more than 5,000 years by the Native Americans. Sunflower seeds are an excellent source of Vitamin E, which has significant anti-inflammatory effects that result in the reduction of symptoms in asthma and osteoarthritis. Sunflower seeds are rich sources of magnesium and selenium as well. Magnesium is necessary for healthy bones and energy production. Numerous studies have demonstrated that sunflower seeds play an important role in the prevention of cardiovascular disease and rheumatoid arthritis. They have been shown to lower high blood pressure, prevent migraine headaches, reduce the risk of heart attack and stroke, reduce the development of diabetic complications, and even reduce the risk of certain cancers. This superfood can even help decrease the severity and frequency of hot flashes in women going through menopause.

DRIED MUSHROOMS
Mushrooms are not high in protein but I put them in this section because they can be used as a meat substitute and they are a good source of Zinc and Vitamin D.

Tips on Using Seeds
Flax, hemp, sesame, and pumpkin seeds can be ground in a spice grinder then sprinkled over rice, cereal, salad, cous cous or used as a homemade protein powder.

They fall roughly into two categories:
Asian mushrooms *like shiitake, wood ear, cloud ear, and matsutake*
European/American mushrooms *like porcini, morel, trumpet, oyster, portabello and chanterelle.*

Asian mushrooms tend to be stronger in flavor than European/American. I like the European/American mushrooms better for meat substitutions because their flavor does not overpower the seasonings but shiitake can also work well. Dried mushrooms can be expensive unless you get them from a farmer's market or international market, so check around for the best prices.
They will last a very long time – a year, if not more – if kept in a well-sealed container.

Soaking 'Shrooms
The best way to reconstitute dried mushrooms is to simply soak them in water. Many recipes call for hot or warm water but it isn't always necessary to use hot water. Room temperature water will also soften the mushrooms and many people believe it extracts less of the flavor from the mushrooms, leaving more of the mushroom flavor right there in the mushroom where it belongs. Some mushrooms will have a bit of grit or dirt on them but most is released into the soaking water and will have fallen to the bottom of the bowl. You do not want to add this grit to your dish so either pour it carefully out, leaving the heavier grit in the bowl or strain your broth through a coffee filter or paper towel. I like to strain it, that way I am sure all the grit is left behind.

FATS AND OILS
Fat is a nutrient we need for energy and to metabolize fat-soluble vitamins (Vitamins A, E, D & K). Oils are liquid fat. We need a mix of essential fatty acids, monounsaturated, polyunsaturated, and saturated fat every day to keep our hair, skin and nails healthy, and our joints, nerves and body lubricated and running smoothly. For vegans, fats are found in nuts, avocados, seeds, olives, and oils.

What oil should I be using?
Cooking with oils that have been used for centuries in cultures that have little or no evidence of the

heart disease and cancer that is in our modern societies seems to make sense. Freshly pressed oil is optimal but not always a realistic option, so second best is using unrefined, expeller-pressed or cold pressed organic oils.

How are oils processed?
Cooking oil extraction and refinement are separate processes. Extraction first removes the oil, typically from a seed, nut, or fruit. Refinement then alters the appearance, texture, taste, smell, or stability of the oil.

Expeller pressing oils squeezes the oil source in a mechanical press. The press does not apply any heat on the oil source or expelled oil. If the oil source is a hard-shelled nut or seed, the force of friction in the high-pressure machine may raise the temperature of the oil as it is extracted.

Cold-pressing oils is commonly used for heat-sensitive oils and uses the same mechanical press as expeller-pressing but in a closely temperature-controlled setting, keeping the temperature that the oil is exposed to strictly below 120 degrees Fahrenheit. The controlled temperature keeps heat exposure from changing the oil's subtle flavor. The result is a product, which maintains the highest possible level of flavor, aroma, color and nutritional richness.

Unrefined oils are filtered using a non-chemical process, which only lightly removes large particles. Some, such as sesame or olive oil, may appear cloudy or have visible sediment after sitting. This does not compromise quality. Unrefined oils have more pronounced flavors, colors and fragrances than refined oils. Like unrefined whole grain flours, unrefined oils are more nutritious and have a shorter storage life than refined.

Refined oils are more thoroughly filtered and strained than unrefined, usually with some additional heat and sometimes with the use of harsh chemicals. Refining reduces the nutrient level and flavor.

HEALTHIEST OILS
Olive Oil is monounsaturated oil that should be kept in a dark container to retain nutrients and keep

from going rancid (bad). Extra virgin olive oil should be used on very low heat cooking or not cooked at all due to its low smoke point. The smoke point is the temperature at which oil begins to smoke. When the oil has exceeded its smoke point it has been damaged and potentially harmful free radicals and cancer-causing properties are formed.

Sesame Oil has been used for more than 5,000 years in Asia and can be used for medium-high heat cooking. Sesame oil is one of the most stable vegetable oils, and owes its long shelf life to the high level of natural antioxidants it contains.

Palm Oil has been used in Africa for centuries for deep-frying and high heat frying. It received a bad rap in the U.S. when the fad of "no saturated fats" was going on. But now saturated fats, like palm and coconut, are becoming popular again. Red palm oil is high in beta-carotene and reduces blood cholesterol. White palm oil is made by boiling the red palm oil and is rich in antioxidants. White palm oil can be found as vegan shortening.

Peanut Oil is a monounsaturated fat that has been used in Africa and Asia for centuries. It can be used in medium-high heat cooking. Peanuts are a common food allergen so obviously peanut oil should not be given to anyone with a peanut allergy.

Coconut Oil is a saturated fat that has been shown to help strengthen immunity and increase energy. It can be used for high heat cooking, pan frying and baking. It also has a light buttery flavor and has become one of the main oils I use but **it should not be used for people with a tree nut allergy.** *Coconut oil has a very strong flavor so please use in small amounts or along with coconut milk until you get used to the flavor.*

Flax Seed Oil and **Hemp Oil** are very high in healthy Omega-3 and Omega-6 fats. These oils are very unstable and can go bad easily when extracted from the seed, so it should come in a dark bottle and be kept in the refrigerator. These oils should never be heated or used in cooking.

Toasted Sesame Oil is dark brown and has a distinctive nutty flavor. It is made from toasted sesame seeds and should not be confused with regular sesame oil. This has become one of my favorite oils as

a substitute for soy sauce to give foods an amazing Asian flavor. A small amount goes a long way to add a rich flavor to your meals.

NATURAL SWEETENERS

Natural sweeteners can be a healthy alternative to white sugar because they have more nutrients, but keep in mind that too much of any sweetener can be harmful to your health. Moderation is key!

Agave Nectar is syrup from a cactus type plant. It tastes like a mix of honey and maple syrup and can be used as a replacement for both. It has a very low glycemic index (does not raise blood sugar to high levels), so that makes it wonderful for diabetics. Agave has trace amounts of calcium, magnesium, and potassium. Raw agave is best because it has gone through less processing and retains more of its nutrients than the non-raw variety.

Maple syrup is made by heating the sap from maple trees. It is high in potassium, calcium, and B vitamins. Make sure to use 100% pure maple syrup to avoid artificial ingredients and high fructose corn syrup.

Honey is not considered vegan in all circles because it is made from bees. But it is a natural sweetener and usually less expensive than agave or maple syrup. Many vegans still use honey because of its healing properties and its high level of amino acids, calcium, potassium, and phosphorus. It can be substituted for agave or maple syrup in these recipes.

Brown Rice Syrup is made from rice and has a mild light taste. It's not as sweet as other sweeteners so it's great for diabetics.

Black Strap Molasses is the syrup resulting from the processing of sugar. It's basically made of all of the nutrients that have been removed from white sugar. It's very high in iron and calcium. Because of its strong flavor, molasses can be used along with maple syrup and agave and should not be used alone unless you are used to it.

Stevia is an herb that has a naturally sweet flavor. The natural herb form helps to regulate blood sugar,

soothes the intestines and stomach, and helps to prevent tooth decay. It comes in powdered, liquid, or herbal forms and tastes similar to Equal™.

Coconut sugar also called Coconut Palm Sugar, is made from the sap of the coconut plant. It has a moderately low glycemic index (does not raise blood sugar to high levels) and retains quite a bit of the nutrients found in the coconut palm. It contains minerals such as iron, zinc, calcium and potassium, along with some fatty acids, that may provide some health benefits. Coconut sugar makes baked goods very moist and can be used as a substitute for brown sugar.

Sucanat is made by boiling all of the water out of sugar cane. It is less processed than evaporated cane juice and turbinado (raw sugar) and it still contains trace amounts of the vitamins and nutrients because it has not been stripped of its color. Sucanat costs the least among the more nutritious natural sweeteners and is great for baking. Sucanat has minimal amounts of potassium, vitamin A, calcium, magnesium and other minerals. I've been seeing a "white" version of sucanat in stores lately but the darker it is, the better.

NON-DAIRY OPTIONS

Mayo: Non-dairy mayonnaise is made from a mix of oil and some type of protein. There are brands that have soy-free options that are really tasty as well.

Milk: There are a variety of non-dairy milks such as soy, almond, hemp, flax, rice, and coconut, just to name a few. I only use unsweetened milk because I don't like to add unnecessary sugar to my family's diet. I also used only unsweetened non-dairy milk for the recipes in this book. Using sweetened milk will make savory dishes too sweet and baked goods sweeter than you might like. Feel free to choose your favorite kinds for these recipes because they can easily be interchanged.

Margarine: Non-dairy margarine is made from a mix of different vegetable oils and adds a nice buttery

Honey and Young Children

Do not give honey to children under the age of two years because their digestive systems are not mature enough to digest a bacteria present in honey, which could cause a serious illness called botulism.

flavor to foods. Some contain hydrogenated oils (or trans fats) so please read your labels and avoid those. Coconut oil and vegan shortening (palm oil) can also be used as butter substitutions but will give your food a slightly different flavor than margarine.

Egg Substitutions

Eggs provide structure, texture and binding for baked goods. When baking vegan and gluten-free, the trick is get the baked items to rise and to be moist. Below are the egg substitutes used in this book.

Flax seeds contain ingredients that can form a gel, when combined with liquids, and can work to either emulsify, stick things together, or soften foods. Flax seed gel imitates many things that eggs do in traditional baking applications. They cannot be used for things like meringues but can easily be substituted in foods like cookies and muffins.

I also like to use flax seeds instead of xanthum gum in gluten-free baking. If possible, purchase flax seeds whole, then grind a small amount yourself with a coffee/spice grinder. After you grind them, store them in an airtight container in your refrigerator/freezer where they will keep for about a month. If using flax seeds while baking, note that the brown variety will be more likely to darken your baked goods due their brown hulls. If you prefer, try to find the golden ones so that you cannot see the flecks of seeds in your baked goods.

Chia seeds work similarly to flax seeds where they form a gel and pull ingredients together when heated. I like to use flax seeds along with chia for added emulsification and rising. I also like to use chia instead of xanthum gum as a stabilizer in gluten-free baking. White chia seeds are less visible than the darker varieties and will be less visible in your finished product but they can be difficult to find.

Ener-G Egg Replacer is an old school brand of egg substitution made from a mix of different starches. It works awesome and does not change the taste or texture of baked goods. It can be difficult to find sometimes but is usually found in health foods stores and sometimes in the natural food section of traditional grocery stores. If you can't find it locally this is one product worth purchasing online.

SPICES AND SEASONINGS

There are a variety of spices used in this book because there are many different cuisines represented. Don't shy away from stocking up your spice pantry because that's what helps the food taste so good!

Ancho chili

Amchoor powder (mango)

Allspice

Bay leaf

Black pepper

Basil

Chili garlic sauce

Cumin

Coriander

Cayenne

Chili powder

Cardamom

Cinnamon

Cloves

Curry powder, yellow

Fennel

Fenugreek

Granulated garlic/ garlic powder

Ginger

Garam masala

Italian seasoning

Kefir lime leaves

Lemongrass

Mirin – rice cooking wine

Nutmeg

Oregano

Onion powder/ granulated onion

Paprika, regular

Paprika, smoked

Red pepper flakes

Sage

Sea salt

Toasted Sesame oil

Thai red curry paste

Thyme

Turmeric

What's the difference in paprika?

Regular paprika is the most commonly found and is a blend of sweet and hot varieties and has a relatively neutral flavor. It's great for adding color to your dishes or as a garnish.

Sweet paprika (commonly labeled as Hungarian sweet paprika) has a rich, fruity flavor like a red bell pepper with no heat. It's great as an all-around paprika and more interesting than the regular stuff.

Spanish smoked paprika is made from dried chilies that are smoked over oak giving the spice a woodsy, smoky flavor that is great for stews and roast meats. In vegan cooking it can give a meaty flavor.

COOKING WITH LEMONGRASS

To use fresh lemon grass, remove the tough, outer leaves. Simply cut the yellow stalk (A) into 2-3 inch lengths (B). Next, "bruise" these sections by bending them several times or banging them with the handle of your knife (C).

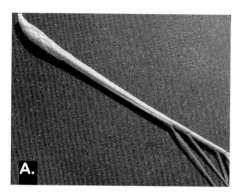
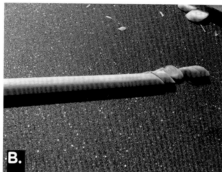
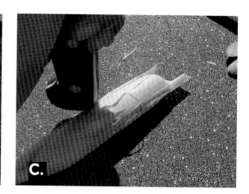

VEGAN AND ALLERGY FRIENDLY BRANDS

I usually don't mention specific brands in my recipes because it may not always be possible to find all brands in every city. For many companies, brand quality often changes over time and many brands come out for a while and then may go out of business. Also, there are always new brands coming out. But, for this book, some recipes are just easier to make and taste better with certain brands. If you can't find a brand in your city, some are available for order on the internet. Please feel free to use some of your favorites as well. Here are a few of my favorites.

Daiya non-dairy cheese
Sunshine Burger soy free and gluten-free veggie burgers
Amy's soy free and gluten free veggie burgers
Hilary's veggie burgers and patties
Tinkyada gluten free brown rice pasta
Earth Balance soy free non-dairy margarine and mayonnaise
Bob's all-purpose gluten free flour
Spectrum soy free non-dairy mayonnaise

Wild Wood sprouted tofu
Good Karma flax milk
Silk almond milk
Thai Kitchen red curry paste
Huy Fong chili garlic sauce
Miso Master chickpea miso
Enjoy Life chocolate chips
Living Harvest hemp tofu
Coconut Secret coconut aminos

THE VEGAN REMIX
THE PLAYLISTS

Music to cook to, to eat to, to love to. Get inspired for your global journey through food with a selection of my favorite jams I like to rock out to everytime I step into my kitchen.

TURNT UP

1. **FLY AWAY**
   Lenny Kravitz

2. **BRING ME TO LIFE**
   Evanescence

3. **PUT ON**
   Young Jeezy

4. **RADIOACTIVE (REMIX)**
   Imagine Dragons and Kendrick Lamar

5. **MY SONG KNOW WHAT YOU DID IN THE DARK**
   Fall Out Boy

6. **TURN DOWN FOR WHAT**
   DJ Snake and Lil Jon

7. **BIRTHDAY SONG**
   2 Chainz

8. **STARTED FROM THE BOTTOM**
   Drake

9. **WE STILL IN THIS BITCH**
   B.O.B

10. **HIP HOP**
    Dead Prez

RIDE OUT

1. **GUST OF WIND**
   Pharrell Williams

2. **OCEANS**
   Jay Z

3. **IT COULD BE SWEET**
   Portishead

4. **CALIFORNICATION**
   Red Hot Chili Peppers

5. **TIME**
   Jungle

6. **BITCH DON'T KILL MY VIBE (REMIX)**
   Kendrick Lamar and Jay Z

7. **HELLO**
   T.I. featuring Ceelo

8. **REBEL MUSIC**
   Bob Marley

9. **NOTHIN BUT A G THANG**
   Dr. Dre feat. Snoop Dogg

10. **LOOSE ENDS**
    Hanging On A String

POSITIVE VIBES

1. **BLESSED**
   Jill Scott

2. **LEARNING GROWING CHANGING**
   Dead Prez

3. **I KEEP**
   Jill Scott

4. **CLOSER**
   Goapele

5. **LIFE AINT EVER BEEN BETTER**
   Lenny Kravitz

6. **FREE YOUR DREAMS**
   Snarky Puppy featuring Chantae Cann

7. **DOING IT RIGHT**
   Daft Punk

8. **I'M EVERY WOMAN**
   Chaka Khan

9. **THE ANSWER**
   Rahael Saadiq

10. **WE'RE GONNA MAKE IT**
    Damian Marley

11. **WAITING ON THE WORLD TO CHANGE**
    John Mayer

12. **YOU ARE THE SUNSHINE OF MY LIFE**
    Stevie Wonder

SUNDAY MORNING

1. **SPACE COWBOY**
   Jamiroquai

2. **EVERYBODY LOVES THE SUNSHINE**
   Roy Ayers

3. **The Awakening**
   Dead Prez

4. **Green Garden**
   Laura Mvula

5. **Be Water**
   Kendrick Scott Oracle

6. **Cherish The Day**
   Robert Glasper featuring Laylah Hathaway

7. **Crash Into Me**
   Dave Mathews Band

8. **Radio Song**
   Esperanza Spalding

9. **Umi Says**
   Most Def

10. **Makeda**
    Les Nubians

11. **Water No Get Enemy**
    Fela

12. **A Love Supreme**
    John Coltrane

BALL SO HARD

1. **NI**AS IN PARIS**
   Kanye West

2. **POUND CAKE**
   Drake

3. **CAN'T TELL ME NOTHING**
   Kanye West

4. **GO GET IT**
   T.I.

5. **I JUST WANNA BE SUCCESSFUL**
   Drake

6. **HUSSEL**
   M.I.A

7. **U.O.E.N.O.**
   Rocko Featuring Future and 2 Chains

8. **HOW I'M RAISED**
   Ace Hood

9. **F*CKWITHMEYOUKNOWIGOTIT**
   Jay Z featuring Rick Ross

10. **LUXURIOUS**
    Gwen Stefani

11. **POUR IT UP**
    Rihanna

GROWN FOLKS

1. **FOREVER**
   Little Dragon

2. **CROWN ROYAL**
   Jill Scott

3. **PARTITION**
   Beyonce

4. **GOOD LUCK CHARM**
   Ohio Players

5. **LETS STAY TOGETHER**
   Al Green

6. **GIVE ME YOUR LOVE**
   Curtis Mayfield

7. **DON'T YOU WANNA STAY**
   Bill Withers

8. **NOTHING CAN COME BETWEEN US**
   Sade

9. **LOVE IS MORE THAN A WEDDING DAY**
   Cody Chesnutt

10. **ALICIA KEYS**
    Unthinkable

11. **KISS FROM A ROSE**
    Seal

OLD SKOOL

1. **BEEF**
   KRS-One

2. **BE HEALTHY**
   Dead Prez

3. **KING OF ROCK**
   RUN D.M.C

4. **UPSIDE DOWN**
   Diana Ross

5. **I'M YOUR PUSHERMAN**
   Ice T

6. **SOUL FOOD**
   Goodie Mob

7. **CHANGES**
   2Pac

8. **AFRICA**
   Toto

9. **DUB MARCUS SAY**
   Steel Pulse

10. **BABY I'M SCARED OF YOU**
    Womak and Womack

11. **THE MESSAGE**
    Grand Master Flash and the Furious Five

ORGANIC PLAYERS
NON GMO

clockwise from left:
Fruit Parfait (pg 39);
SpottieOattieDopalicious
Pancakes (pg 47); No nuts,
No Glory Cereal (pg 49)

Seoul to Seoul "Chickn" and Waffles (pg 50)

AFYA IBOMU
THE VEGAN REMIX

EVERYBODY LOVES
GOOD FOOD

THE BREAKFAST CLUB
MORNING GROOVES

breakfast sweet potatoes

fruit parfait

scrambled kale + tofu

fat boys fried biscuits

stack chedda biscuits

coconut pancakes

nana cakes

spottieoattiedopalicious pancakes

cheesy grits

no nuts, no glory cereal

seoul to seoul "chikin" and waffles

good morning

BREAKFAST SWEET POTATOES

SERVES 4 PEOPLE

Soy Free, Gluten Free,
Dairy Free, Nut Free, Grain Free

Ingredients:

2 large sweet potatoes cut into 1-inch cubes

3 tablespoons oil, divided

1/2 cup red onion, chopped

1/2 cup red bell pepper, chopped

2 cloves garlic, chopped

1 teaspoon sea salt

1/2 teaspoon black pepper

2 tablespoons fresh rosemary chopped
or 1/2 teaspoon dried

Directions:

1. Cut potatoes into cubes and heat a large cast iron or non-stick skillet over medium heat.
2. Add oil and potatoes to the pan and lay flat. Cook on that side for 5 minutes. Turn potatoes over and cook on the other side for 5 minutes.
3. Repeat step 2 one more time and the potatoes should begin to soften.
4. Increase heat to medium-high and add the red onions, bell peppers, and garlic, sauté until tender, 5 to 6 minutes. Potatoes should begin to get golden and crisp.
5. Season with salt, pepper and rosemary cook for 1-2 more minutes and serve.

FRUIT PARFAIT

**MAKES 4 PARFAITS
& 1 CUP OF WHIPPED CREAM**

Soy Free, Gluten Free, Dairy Free,
Grain Free

Ingredients:

1½ cup pineapple, chopped

1½ cup kiwi, sliced

1½ cup berries

1½ cup grapes

Fruit Options: Melons, peaches, nectarines, and oranges

Easy Coconut Whipped Cream Ingredients:

1 can of full-fat coconut milk

1 tablespoon agave or maple syrup

1/2 teaspoon vanilla (optional)

Directions:

1. Place can of coconut milk in the fridge overnight. It needs to be chilled until it's very firm.
2. Just before you make your whipped cream, place a large mixing bowl in the freezer for about 5 minutes.
3. Remove the chilled can of milk from fridge and carefully flip it upside down and open the can. The liquid coconut water (the part that doesn't harden) will now be at the top of the can.
4. Pour the coconut liquid into another bowl. Don't throw it away; it can be used in smoothies and cooking.
5. Scoop the coconut cream into your chilled bowl and using a hand mixer, whip the cream until fluffy.
6. Add agave and vanilla then whip it again until well mixed. Put in the refrigerator until you are done cutting the fruit.
7. Cut the fruit in bite size pieces and either mix the fruit together or keep separate.
8. Then layer the mixed fruit or each individual type of fruit in a glass.
9. Add about 2-3 tablespoons of whipped cream in between each layer. Top with a scoop of cream. Repeat for the remaining glasses

*Keep one or two cans of coconut milk in the back of the fridge just in case, so that you can make a quick whipped cream at any time. Also some companies are making their milk where the water will not separate from the cream, so keep in mind you may need to try a few different brands first.

SCRAMBLED KALE + TOFU

SERVES 4 PEOPLE

Gluten Free, Dairy Free,
Nut Free, Grain Free,
Soy Free if Hemp Tofu is used

Ingredients:

2 tablespoons oil
1 block extra firm tofu
3 cups shredded kale**
1 teaspoon smoked paprika
1/2 cup chopped onions
1 tablespoon minced garlic
1 1/4 teaspoon sea salt or to taste
2 teaspoons granulated garlic or garlic powder
1/4 cup low sodium vegetable broth

Directions:

1. Heat a medium cast iron or non-stick pan on medium heat. Add oil and crumble tofu into the pan.
2. Lay flat and cook for about 5 minutes browning lightly. Then flip over, lay flat and cook for 5 more minutes.
3. Add all ingredients except veggie broth, sauté for two minutes. Then add broth, cook 5 more minutes oruntil kale is at desired consistency.

**Kale can be substituted for broccoli, chard or spinach

FAT BOYS FRIED BISCUITS

MAKES 7-8 BISCUITS

Soy Free, Gluten Free,
Dairy Free, Nut Free

Dry Ingredients:
1 cup all-purpose gluten free flour
1 teaspoon baking powder
1/4 teaspoon sea salt

Wet Ingredients:
2 tablespoons oil
6 tablespoons unsweetened non-dairy milk
3 teaspoons agave or maple syrup
Enough oil for frying, about 1/2 cup

Directions:
1. Mix dry ingredients into a medium bowl. Mix wet ingredients in a small bowl.
2. Mix wet into dry, do not over mix. Batter will be slightly lumpy. Let sit for 5-10 minutes.
3. Heat a medium sized pan on medium-low heat and add oil. Scoop a heaping tablespoon of batter for each biscuit and fry on both sides until golden brown.
4. Strain on paper towels and serve warm.

STACK CHEDDA BISCUITS

MAKES 12 BISCUITS

Soy Free, Gluten Free,
Dairy Free, Nut Free

Wet Ingredients:

1 cup unsweetened non-dairy milk

1 tablespoon apple cider vinegar

2 teaspoons vanilla extract

6 tablespoons non-dairy margarine, cold and cut into small cubes

Dry Ingredients:

2 cups all-purpose gluten free flour

1/2 teaspoon sea salt

1 tablespoon baking powder

1/4 teaspoon granulated garlic or powder

1 tablespoon flax seed meal

3/4 cup non-dairy cheddar style cheese

Topping:

3 tablespoons vegan margarine

1/2 teaspoon dried parsley

1/4 teaspoon granulated garlic

Pinch of sea salt

Directions:

1. Preheat oven to 400°F. Line a large baking sheet with parchment paper.
2. In a small bowl mix the milk, vinegar and vanilla. Let sit for at least 5-10 minutes.
3. In a large bowl or food processor mix all the dry ingredients except the cheese.
4. Use a food processor or 2 knives used scissor fashion to cut the margarine in the dry ingredients until small pea-sized crumbs form.
5. Remove from food processor, add the cheese and toss until coated with flour.
6. Add the liquid mixture and stir until just combined—don't over mix.
7. Place 1/4 cup full-drops onto the baking sheet about 2 inches apart.
8. Bake 14-16 minutes until golden around the edges. In a small pot heat the margarine for the topping on low just until melted. Turn off and add the parsley, garlic and sea salt.
9. Remove the biscuits from the oven and brush topping mix generously over the top of biscuits while hot. Best served warm.

COCONUT PANCAKES

MAKES 10-12 PANCAKES

Soy Free, Gluten Free, Dairy Free

Dry Ingredients:

1 1/4 cup all purpose gluten free flour

1 tablespoon flax seed meal

2 teaspoons baking powder

1/4 teaspoon sea salt

1/4 teaspoon baking soda

1/3 cup shredded unsweetened coconut flakes

Wet Ingredients:

1 cup coconut milk

1 tablespoon apple cider vinegar

2 tablespoons olive or coconut oil**

1 tablespoon maple syrup

1 tablespoon vanilla extract

Directions:

1. Mix coconut milk and vinegar in a medium bowl, sit to the side for at least 5 minutes.
2. Mix dry ingredients together in a small bowl.
3. Add remaining wet ingredients to the coconut milk.
4. Whisk the dry ingredients a third at a time into the wet ingredients. Whisk for about 30 seconds. Batter should be slightly lumpy. Let rest for 5-10 minutes.
5. Heat a cast iron/non-stick pan or griddle to a medium-low heat. It's hot enough when water drops on it, turns to beads and bounces across griddle.
6. Oil griddle very lightly and pour some of the pancake mix into a medium round on the pan.
7. When you see bubbles forming on top, flip the cake. Cook for a minute or two until done.
8. Continue to lightly oil the pan every other pancake. The first 1 or 2 pancakes usually don't come out well, so don't get discouraged!

**If using coconut oil, make sure all wet ingredients are at room temperature or else oil will solidify.

NANA CAKES

MAKES 10-12 PANCAKES

Soy Free, Gluten Free,
Dairy Free, Nut Free

Dry Ingredients:

1¼ cup of all-purpose gluten free flour

2 teaspoons baking powder

1 teaspoon cinnamon

1 tablespoon flax seed meal

Pinch of salt

1/4 cup walnuts, pecans or pumpkin seeds,
chopped (optional)

Wet Ingredients:

2 ripe bananas mashed, about 1 cup

2 tablespoons oil

2 tablespoons maple syrup

1/2 teaspoon vanilla

1 to 1¼ cup unsweetened non-dairy milk

Directions:

1. Mix dry ingredients together in a medium bowl. Set to the side.
2. Mash the bananas in a small bowl until there are no lumps, or very few. Then add the remaining wet ingredients and mix well. The more milk you add, the thinner the pancakes will be.
3. Make a hole in the center of dry ingredients, pour in wet ingredients and mix. The batter should be a little lumpy. Let the batter rest for 5-10 minutes.
4. Heat a cast iron/non-stick pan or griddle to a medium-low heat. It's hot enough when water drops on it, turns to beads and bounces across griddle.
5. Oil a griddle very lightly and pour some of the pancake mix into a medium round on the pan.
6. When you see bubbles forming on top, flip the cake. Cook for 1-2 minutes to brown pancake on the other side.
7. Continue to lightly oil the pan every other pancake. The first 1 or 2 pancakes usually don't come out well so don't get discouraged!

SPOTTIEOATTIEDOPALICIOUS PANCAKES

MAKES 8-10 PANCAKES
Soy Free, Gluten Free, Dairy Free

Dry Ingredients:

1 1/4 cup all purpose gluten free flour
1/2 cup gluten free granola
1 tablespoon flax seed meal
2 teaspoons baking powder
1/4 teaspoon sea salt

Wet Ingredients:

2 tablespoons oil
1 cup unsweetened non-dairy milk
2 tablespoons maple syrup
1 tablespoon vanilla
1/3 cup blue berries, fresh or frozen

Directions:

1. If the berries are frozen, quickly run under cold water to defrost, then drain.
2. Mix dry ingredients together in a medium bowl. Sit to the side.
3. Mix all the wet ingredients in a small bowl, except the blueberries.
4. Make a hole in the center of dry ingredients, pour in wet ingredients and mix. The batter should be
   a little lumpy. Add blueberries and lightly fold into batter. Do not over mix. Then let the batter rest for 5- 10 minutes.
5. Heat a cast iron/non-stick pan or griddle to a medium-low heat. It's hot enough when water drops on it, turns to beads and bounces across griddle.
6. Oil griddle very lightly and pour pancake mix into a medium round on the pan.
7. When you see bubbles forming on top, flip the cake. Cook for a minute or two to brown on the other side.
8. Continue to lightly oil the pan every other pancake. The first 1 or 2 pancakes usually don't come out well, so don't get discouraged!

CHEESY GRITS

SERVES 4-6 PEOPLE

Soy Free, Gluten Free,
Dairy Free, Nut Free

Ingredients:

2 cups unsweetened non-dairy milk

2 cups water

1 1/2 teaspoon sea salt

1 cup organic yellow corn grits

1/4 cup minced onions

1/4 teaspoon black pepper

3 tablespoons non-dairy margarine

1/2 cup non-dairy cheddar style cheese

Directions:

1. Place milk, water, and salt into a large, heavy-bottomed pot over medium-high heat and bring to a light boil.
2. Once the milk mixture comes to a boil, add the onions and gradually add the grits while continually whisking. Once all of the grits have been incorporated, decrease the heat to low and cover.
3. Cook for 15 to 20 minutes or until mixture is creamy.
4. Remove lid and whisk every 3 to 4 minutes to prevent grits from sticking or forming lumps. Be sure to get into corners of pot when whisking.
5. Remove from the heat, add the pepper and margarine, and whisk to combine.
6. Once the margarine is melted, gradually whisk in the cheese a little at a time. Serve immediately.

NO NUTS, NO GLORY CEREAL

Dry Ingredients:

1 1/2 cups gluten free rolled oats

1/4 teaspoon kosher salt

1/2 cup crispy brown rice cereal

2 tablespoons hemp seeds

1/4 cup raw pumpkin seeds

1/4 teaspoon baking soda

2 tablespoons flax seed meal

1 teaspoon cinnamon

1/4 teaspoon nutmeg

1/2 cup coconut sugar

1/2 cup raisins

Wet Ingredients:

3 tablespoons unsweetened non dairy milk + 1/2 teaspoon chia seeds

1/3 cup maple syrup

2 tablespoons neutral oil, such as olive or grape seed

3/4 teaspoon vanilla extract

Directions:

1. Preheat the oven to 375°F and line a cookie sheet with parchment paper or lightly oil it.
2. Mix milk and chia seeds and sit to the side
3. Mix all dry ingredients in a large bowl except raisins.
4. Mix wet ingredients into a small bowl.
5. Mix chia seed mixture as well as wet and dry ingredients together then lay out flat on the cookie sheet and bake for 15-18 minutes.
6. Take out once the granola gets golden brown then add raisins and lightly mix.
7. Let cool completely and store in a glass container.

SEOUL TO SEOUL "CHICKN' AND WAFFLES

Waffles:

2 tablespoons flaxseed meal + 1/4 cup non dairy milk

1 1/2 cup non dairy milk + 1 tablespoon apple cider vinegar

1 3/4 cup all purpose gluten free flour

1/4 cup cornstarch

2 teaspoons baking powder

3 tablespoons sucanat

1/2 teaspoon vanilla

2 tablespoons oil

Korean fried tofu:

Pre Coating:

1/4 cup cornstarch

2 teaspoons sea salt

1/2 teaspoon baking powder

1/4 teaspoon black pepper

1/4 teaspoon granulated garlic

1 block of extra firm tofu

Oil, for frying

Tofu Batter:

1/2 cup cornstarch

1/2 cup all purpose gluten free flour

1/2 teaspoon red chili flakes

1/2 teaspoon sea salt

2 1/2 teaspoons granulated garlic or garlic powder

2 1/2 teaspoons granulated onion or onion powder

1/4 teaspoon baking powder

1 cup water

1/3 cup mirin (rice wine)

Directions:

For Waffles

1. Add flaxseed meal to milk in a small bowl, mix well and sit to the side.
2. Add apple cider vinegar to milk and sit to the side.
3. Mix together the flour, cornstarch, baking powder and sucanat into a large bowl.
4. Add flax mixture, vinegar mixture and remaining ingredients to the dry ingredients and mix well.
5. Let mixture sit for about five minutes and turn on waffle iron on high heat.
6. Lightly oil waffle iron and add 1 cup of waffle batter to iron. Close and cook until lightly brown. My waffle iron has a light that tells me when the waffle is done. I usually cook my waffle about 2-3 minutes longer until lightly golden brown.

SERVES 4 PEOPLE

Gluten free, dairy free, nut free, can be soy free if hemp tofu is used.

7. Remove waffle and let cool on a wire rack to keep it crispy.
8. Repeat steps 6-7 for remaining waffles.

For Tofu:

1. Make the pre-coating: In a large bowl, whisk together the first 5 ingredients. Add the tofu and toss well until evenly coated in all areas. Transfer the tofu to a rack, shaking it well to get rid of any excess coating. Let rest uncovered for 1 hour.
2. Pour enough oil into a large pot to reach a depth of 2 inches. Heat the oil over medium-high heat until a deep fry thermometer reads 350 degrees.
3. Make the batter: In a large bowl, whisk together the dry ingredients. In a smaller bowl, whisk together the wet ingredients. Just before frying, whisk the wet mixture into the dry mixture. The consistency should be relatively thin and runny.
4. Working in two batches, dip each piece of tofu into the batter, letting excess batter drip off. Suspend the tofu in the oil for a couple of seconds for it to set before letting it slip completely into the oil, otherwise the tofu will fall and stick to the bottom of the pot.
5. Fry tofu until golden brown and cooked through. Transfer to a wire rack to drain.

GOOD MORNING

Ingredients:

1 large apple
1/2 cup soaked raw almond
3 medjool dates, pitted
1/8 teaspoon of cinnamon
1 small squeeze of lemon juice

Directions:

1. Soak almonds over night and strain. Add to food processor and pulse a few times just to lightly chop.

2. Add dates and pulse until well mixed.

3. Lightly chop apple and add along with remaining ingredients to food processor and mix well. Mixture should be well combined but not turned into a paste.

4. Eat immediately.

Ital Stew
(pg 69)

clockwise from top left:
3 Bean Chilli (pg 67);
Asian Corn Soup (pg 70);
Wild Rice Soup (pg 63)

Tom Yum
Soup
(pg 60)

THE VEGAN REMIX

STIR IT UP

SOUPS & STEWS

MUSHROOM BROTH

MAKES ABOUT 4-5 CUPS

**Soy Free, Gluten Free,
Dairy free, Nut Free, Grain Free**

I added this recipe because sometimes it can be difficult to find mushroom broth in stores.

Ingredients:

1 cup dried mushrooms

2 cups vegetable scraps (onion and shallot skins, carrot and celery trimmings, etc.)

1/4 teaspoon dried parsley

1 garlic clove, minced

1 bay leaf

8 cups water

Directions:

1. Combine all ingredients in la arge stock pot and bring to a boil, then reduce heat to low and simmer partially covered for 45 minutes.

2. Remove lid and simmer uncovered for 30 minutes more.

3. Allow stock to cool, then pour through a fine mesh strainer into a bowl.

4. Press vegetable scraps against the strainer with a wooden spoon in order to extract as much stock as possible.

5. Discard solids and store stock in 2 cup servings in a container or freezer bag.

C.R.E.A.M. OF MUSHROOM SOUP

Soy Free, Gluten Free, Dairy free, Nut Free

While growing up my mother would add cream of mushroom soup to rice, veggies, casseroles, or just about anything. I have yet to find a non-dairy pre-made cream of mushroom soup, which inspired this recipe. Enjoy!

Ingredients:

1/2 cup of non-dairy margarine

1/2 cup of finely minced onion

1/4 cup of finely minced celery

2 cups finely minced fresh mushrooms

(button, white or portobello)

2 teaspoon of sea salt

3/4 cup of all-purpose gluten free flour

2 cups of mushroom or low sodium vegetable broth

2 cups unsweetened non-dairy milk

Directions:

1. Melt the margarine in a large skillet and sauté the onion and celery over medium heat until tender, but not browned.

2. Stir in the chopped mushrooms and salt; stir and cook about 2-3 minutes.

3. Stir in the flour a little at a time until fully incorporated, cook about 4 minutes, stirring constantly.

4. Increase heat to medium-high and slowly add the broth a little at a time, until fully incorporated.

5. Reduce heat to low and slowly stir in milk.

6. Simmer for about 15 minutes or until thickened.

Use about 1¼ cups of soup to replace 1 can of soup. The recipe makes a little over 4 cups, or *roughly* enough to equal about 4 cans.

Use any place where you would use Campbell's ® Condensed Cream of Mushroom Soup. Soup can be frozen into individual servings.

TOM YUM

SERVES 4-6 PEOPLE

Soy Free, Gluten Free,
Dairy Free, Nut Free, Grain Free

Veggies:

2 tablespoons oil

2 stalks lemon grass including bulb end, smashed and cut into 2-3 pieces**

2 inch piece ginger or galanga, sliced

1 tablespoon garlic, minced

1/2 cup onion, chopped

1 1/2 cup tomatoes, diced

1 cup button mushrooms, chopped

1 cup snow peas cut in half

1 cup baby corn or 1 cup frozen corn

Optional veggies add 1-2 cups of any of these: green beans, bok choy, cabbage, and cauliflower

Optional protein choices: chickpeas, extra firm tofu

Broth:

3 cups low sodium vegetable broth

5-7 cups water, divided

5 keffir lime leaves (optional)

3 teaspoons toasted sesame oil

Spices:

1/2 teaspoon chili garlic sauce

3 teaspoons sea salt

** See page 28 for cooking with lemongrass

2 tablespoons fresh cilantro (6 sprigs) or 1/2 teaspoon dried

Juice of 2 limes or lemons

Garnish:

Green onions (optional)

Serve with rice or rice noodles

Directions:

1. If using tofu, cut into steaks, pan fry in oil and add to soup in step 5.

2. In a medium soup pot, sauté ginger, onions, lemongrass and garlic for about 3 minutes then add tomatoes.

3. Cover for 5 minutes on medium-low heat, stirring occasionally. Veggies will start to caramelize.

4. Have 2 cups of water handy at the end of 5 minutes to prevent burning.

5. Add broth ingredients, your protein option, spices and remaining veggies except snow peas and bok choy then bring soup to a boil. The amount of veggies you add will determine the amount of water you use.

6. Reduce heat to medium-low and simmer for 20 minutes.

7. Add snow peas and bok choy in the last 5 minutes of cooking.

MISO HUNGRY

SERVES 4-6 PEOPLE
Soy Free, Gluten Free,
Dairy Free, Nut Free, Grain Free,
can be Soy Free

Ingredients:
1 tablespoon oil
1 can chickpeas or 4 oz tofu cut into steaks
1 inch to 3 inch strip of kelp (kombu)
1/4 cup chickpea miso

Veggies:
1/2 cup chopped onions
2 tablespoons minced garlic
1 cup carrots, chopped
1/2 cup corn kernels
1/2 cup celery, chopped
3/4 cup green beans or broccoli, chopped

Broth:
1 tablespoon toasted sesame oil
6 cups of water
1 cup low sodium vegetable broth
2 teaspoon sea salt

Directions:
1. If using tofu, cut into steaks and pan fry in a soup pot with oil on a medium-high heat until brown on both sides.
2. Add vegetables and sauté until soft, about 5 minutes. Tofu should break up into bite size pieces.
3. Add chickpeas and broth ingredients then bring to a boil.
4. Lower heat, cut kelp into thin bite sized strips, add and simmer for 15 minutes.
5. Turn soup off.
6. Skim off 1 cup of stock and dissolve miso into it, then add back to the soup and mix well.
7. Ladle into bowls and serve.

WILD RICE SOUP

SERVES 6 PEOPLE

Soy free, Gluten free,
Dairy free, Nut free

Ingredients:
1 cup wild rice
2 1/2 cups water

Veggies:
2 tablespoons non-dairy margarine or oil
1 cup rutabaga, cubed
1/3 cup onion, chopped
1/2 cup chopped celery
1/4 cup chopped green pepper
2 cloves garlic, minced
1 cup chopped fresh button mushrooms

Spices:
1 1/4 teaspoon black pepper (or to taste)
1 teaspoon granulated garlic
2 teaspoons sea salt
2 1/2 tablespoons whole sage, divided
1 1/2 cup mushroom broth
8 cups of water
2 cups unsweetened non-dairy milk
1 cup non-dairy cheddar cheese
1 tablespoon arrowroot or cornstarch + 3 tablespoons milk

Directions:
1. In a medium pot, bring water to a boil and add rice. Cover, turn heat down to medium-low, cover and cook for 30 min.
2. While rice is cooking, in a large pot add margarine and rutabaga, sauté for 5 min.
3. Add remaining veggies and sauté for 5 more minutes.
4. Add pepper, garlic, salt and 2 tablespoons of sage.
5. Add rice and remaining ingredients except arrowroot.
6. Bring to a light boil, then turn down heat to medium and simmer uncovered for 30 minutes.
7. While the soup is cooking, stir for 1 minute every 6 minutes to help thicken soup.
8. Mix arrowroot and milk then add the mixture along with the remaining sage in the last 5 minutes of cooking.

CURRY NOODLE SOUP

Ingredients:
1 box dried pad thai, mei fun or vermicelli noodles
3 tablespoons oil

Veggies:
1/3 cup dried mushrooms in 2/3 cup warm water **
1/2 cup onions, thinly sliced
1 cup carrots, chopped
2 inch piece of ginger, grated
2 garlic cloves, minced
1/4 cup baby corn cut in half
1/2 cup snow peas cut crosswise
1 cup broccoli, chopped small

Optional veggie choices: green beans, cabbage, bok choy, and cauliflower
Optional protein: 1/2 block pan fried tofu or 1 can chickpeas

Spices:
2 tablespoons Thai red curry paste
3 teaspoons yellow curry powder
1 teaspoon ground coriander
1 teaspoon ground turmeric
1 teaspoon granulated garlic or garlic powder

Broth:
2 cups low sodium vegetable broth
One can unsweetened coconut milk
4 cups water
2 teaspoons agave
3 teaspoons sea salt
1/2 teaspoon chili garlic sauce
1 tablespoon toasted sesame oil
Juice of 1 lemon

Garnish:
1/4 cup chopped cilantro leaves
2 scallions, thinly sliced
Lime wedges and sliced chilies

Mushroom tip: Use a mild tasting mushroom like shitake, oyster or chanterelle.

SERVES 6 PEOPLE

**Soy Free, Gluten Free,
Dairy Free**

Directions:

1. Soak the mushrooms in warm water and sit to the side.
2. Heat a medium sized soup pot on medium-low and add oil.
3. Sauté onions, carrots, ginger and garlic for 3-5 minutes until soft.
4. Add spices, protein option and remaining veggies except snow peas and broccoli. Sauté for 3 minutes.
5. Add broth ingredients and mushroom with soaking water and bring soup to a boil.
6. Once soup comes to a boil, reduce heat to medium-low and simmer for 15 minutes.
7. While soup is simmering make the noodles. These noodles usually only take a few minutes to cook.
8. Strain the hot noodle water into a bowl and sit to the side. Rinse the noodles in cold water to stop the cooking process then toss them with a little oil to prevent sticking.
9. Put the broccoli and snow peas in the hot noodle water for about 3 minutes. Just enough time to lightly soften the veggies.
10. Add remaining veggies to the soup in the last 3-5 minutes of cooking.
11. Garnish with cilantro, scallions and lime.

3 BEAN CHILI

SERVES 6-8 PEOPLE

Soy Free, Gluten Free,
Dairy Free, Nut Free, Grain Free

Ingredients:

3 tablespoons of oil
2 tablespoons all purpose gluten free flour
3/4 cup of dry brown or green lentils
1 can black beans
1 can red beans or pinto beans
One 28-oz can of diced tomatoes, with juice
1 1/2 cup low sodium vegetable broth
4 cups water

Vegetables:

1 large onion, chopped
6 cloves to 1 whole bulb of garlic
1/2 cup green peppers, diced
1 cup peeled and chopped winter squash
(kabocha, butternut, delicata, or acorn)
1 cup corn kernels, fresh or frozen

Spices:

2 tablespoons chili powder
2 tablespoons ground ancho chili
2 tablespoons ground coriander
2 tablespoons powdered cumin
1 tablespoon granulated onion
1 tablespoon oregano
2 teaspoons basil
1/2 teaspoon fennel seed
1 1/2 teaspoon sea salt

Directions:

1. Heat a large pot on medium-low heat and add the oil and flour. Mix and cook flour for about 5 minutes making sure it does not burn.
2. Add vegetables and sauté for 5-7 minutes.
3. Add all spices except salt and cook a few minutes. Add remaining ingredients and stir.
4. Bring to a boil then reduce to medium-low heat and cover.
5. Gently cook for a minimum of 30 minutes stirring every 8-10 minutes making sure it does not stick.
6. Add salt and cook for 10 more minutes. Also add more water if needed 1/2 cup at a time.
7. Chili tastes better the longer it sits. Adjust seasoning as desired.

SOUPS AND STEWS · Stir It Up

VEGGIE MEDLEY

SERVES 6-8 PEOPLE

Soy Free, Gluten Free,
Dairy Free, Nut Free, Grain Free

Veggies:

2 tablespoons oil

2 stalks celery, chopped

1 cup onion, chopped

1 cup bell pepper, chopped

3 medium carrots, chopped

2-4 medium potatoes, diced

4 cloves garlic, chopped or 1 1/2 tablespoons minced

1 cup each of at least 2 of these: green peas, corn, rutabaga, cauliflower, green beans (or 2 cups of frozen mixed vegetables)

1 can or 1 1/2 cups of beans (canned or frozen)

Bean options: back-eyed peas, red beans, white beans, chickpeas, lentils, canellini beans

Spices:

1/2 teaspoon black pepper

2 teaspoons sea salt

2 teaspoons granulated garlic or garlic powder

2 teaspoons granulated onion or onion powder

2 teaspoons dry basil or parsley

1 teaspoon oregano

1 inch kelp (kombu)

Broth:

One 15 oz. can crushed tomatoes

8-10 cups water

2 cups low sodium vegetable broth

Juice of 1/2 lemon

Directions:

1. Heat a large soup pot on a medium heat. Add the oil and veggies one at a time and sauté until they are all added, mixing as you are adding each one to prevent sticking.

2. Add spices, stir and cook for a minute. Then add tomatoes, water and veggie broth.

3. Add 8 cups of water. As the soup cooks add more water if necessary.

4. Bring soup to a boil, reduce to medium-low, and cook uncovered for 40 minutes. Stirring occasionally.

5. Right before serving add the juice of 1/2 lemon and stir.

ITAL STEW

SERVES 4-6 PEOPLE

Soy Free, Gluten Free,
Dairy Free

Ingredients:

2 tablespoons oil

3 medium carrots, chopped (about 1 1/2 cups)

3 whole stalks of scallions, with ends cut

3 cloves fresh garlic, about 2 teaspoons minced

1 tablespoon minced or grated ginger

2 medium Idaho potatoes, about 1 1/2 cups

2 cups fresh or frozen corn (cut kernels off cob)

1 green plantain

1 can red beans or black eyed peas

12 medium okra (optional)

5 cups water if no okra, 6 cups with okra

2 cups low sodium vegetable broth

1 cup unsweetened coconut milk

1 tablespoon non-dairy margarine

Juice 1/2 lime or lemon

Dumplings:

1/2 cup all-purpose gluten free flour

1/4 teaspoon baking powder

1/4 teaspoon sea salt

1/8 teaspoon black pepper

2 teaspoons oil

3-4 tablespoons water

Spices:

1 teaspoon ground allspice

12 stalks of fresh thyme or 1/8 teaspoon dried

2 1/2 teaspoons sea salt or to taste

1/2 teaspoon black pepper or to taste

1 small whole Scotch bonnet (habanero) pepper

Directions:

1. Heat a large soup pot on medium-low heat then add oil.

2. Sauté carrots, garlic, scallions and ginger for 5 minutes. Then add potatoes, corn, plantains and beans and sauté for 3-5 minutes.

3. Add all spices except Scotch bonnet and sauté for 30 seconds.

4. Add remaining ingredients and bring soup to a boil, then reduce to medium heat and simmer covered for 20 minutes.

5. While the soup is coming to a boil, mix dumpling ingredients in a small bowl.

6. Start with mixing the flour, baking powder, salt and pepper. Then add oil and 3 tablespoons of water. Do not over mix.
   Dough should be slightly dry. Add extra water if needed, 1 teaspoon at a time.

7. When the soup is turned down to simmer, add dumplings 1 heaping teaspoon at a time.

8. Remove scotch bonnet, scallions and thyme stalks before serving.

ASIAN CORN SOUP

SERVES 4-6 PEOPLE

Soy Free, Gluten Free,
Dairy Free, Nut Free

Veggies:

1 tablespoon oil
4 ears of corn or one 16 oz bag of
frozen, divided
1 cup chopped yellow onion
5 (1/8-inch-thick) slices fresh ginger
1 garlic clove, minced
2 fresh lemongrass stalks, including bulb end,
smashed and cut into 2-3 pieces **
Optional veggies (add up to 2 cups total):
carrots, green beans, and cauliflower

Broth:

8 cups water, divided
2 cups vegetable broth
2 1/2 teaspoons sea salt
Juice of 1 lime or lemon

Spices:

2 tablespoons Asian hot mustard
2 tablespoons of arrowroot or cornstarch
+ 3-4 tablespoons water or low sodium
vegetable broth
1 tablespoon toasted sesame oil
Thinly sliced lime or lemon (optional)

Directions:

1. If using fresh corn, cut corn kernels from ears of corn, set
   aside. Reserve cobs.
2. Heat a large pot over medium-high heat and add oil.
3. Add onion, ginger, lemongrass, garlic and 3 cups of corn to
   pot. Sauté 5 minutes or until tender. Add remaining veggies
   and sauté 3-5 more minutes.
4. Add 6 cups water, vegetable broth, lime juice, corncobs and
   salt; bring to a boil.
5. Add 2 cups water and 1 cup of corn to the blender. Blend
   well then add to the soup.
6. Reduce heat to medium, and simmer 30 minutes.
7. Mix arrowroot and vegetable broth in a small cup.
8. Add arrowroot blend, mustard and sesame oil to the soup
   in the last 10 minutes of cooking.
9. Garnish with lime or lemon.

** See page 27 for cooking with lemongrass

MULLIGATAWNY SOUP

SERVES 4-6 PEOPLE

Soy Free, Gluten Free,
Dairy Free, Nut Free, Grain Free

Ingredients:
10-12 cups water
1 cup yellow split peas

Veggies:
3/4 cup diced tomatoes
2 teaspoons minced garlic
1/4 cup minced onions
1 inch fresh ginger, grated
Juice of 1 1/2 lemons, divided plus the lemons themselves

Spices:
1 1/4 teaspoon ground coriander
1/2 teaspoon turmeric
2 teaspoons sea salt

Garnish:
1/4 cup fresh cilantro

Directions:
1. Add 10 cups of water and peas to a large soup pot and bring to a boil.
2. Cook uncovered on medium-high for 1 hour, stirring occasionally to prevent sticking.
3. Remove from heat and puree in blender or food processor, in batches if necessary.
4. Return to stove and return to a simmer, adding additional water if thinning is needed.
5. Add the juice of 1 lemon plus the lemon itself, the veggies, and all spices except salt. Cook for 15-20 more minutes. Stir occasionally.
6. Turn soup off and add the remaining lemon, lemon juice, salt and cilantro.

Blue Note
Baked Nachos
(pg 92)

clockwise from top:
Summer Rolls (pg 80);
Mariachi Dip (pg 78);
Collard Green Rolls (pg 82)

Sweet Potato
Pizza (pg 90)

EAT-VEG EAT-VEG EAT-VEG EAT-VEG EAT-VEG EAT-VEG EAT-VEG EA
NS ROCK VEGANS ROCK VEGANS ROCK VEGANS ROCK VEGA
EG EAT-VEG EAT-VEG EAT-VEG EAT-VEG EAT-VEG EAT-VEG EA

EAT-VEG EAT-VEG EAT-VEG EAT-VEG EAT-VEG EAT-VEG EA
NS ROCK VEGANS **VEGANS** ROCK VEGANS ROCK VEGA
EG EAT-VEG EAT-VEG EAT-VEG EAT-VEG EAT-VEG EAT-VEG EA
NS ROCK VEGANS ROCK VEGANS **ROCK** VEGANS ROCK VEGA
EG EAT-VEG EAT-VEG EAT-VEG EAT-VEG EAT-VEG EAT-VEG EA
NS ROCK VEGANS ROCK VEGANS ROCK VEGANS ROCK VEGA
EG EAT-VEG EAT-VEG EAT-VEG EAT-VEG EAT-VEG EAT-VEG EA
NS ROCK VEGANS ROCK VEGANS ROCK VEGANS ROCK VEGA
EG EAT-VEG EAT-VEG EAT-VEG EAT-VEG EAT-VEG EAT-VEG EA
NS ROCK VEGANS ROCK VEGANS ROCK VEGANS ROCK VEGA
EG EAT-VEG EAT-VEG EAT-VEG EAT-VEG EAT-VEG EAT-VEG EA
NS ROCK VEGANS ROCK VEGANS ROCK VEGANS ROCK VEGA
EG EAT-VEG EAT-VEG EAT-VEG EAT-VEG EAT-VEG EAT-VEG EA
NS RO CK VEGANS ROCK VEGA
EG EA AT-VEG EAT-VE VEG EA
NS RO CK VEGANS ROC VEGA
EG EA T-VEG EAT-VE VEG EA
NS RO GANS RO VEGA
EG EA T-VEG EAT-VE EA
NS RO VEGANS ROC

OPENING ACTS
WRAPS & SNACKS

MARIACHI DIP

SERVES 4-6 PEOPLE

Gluten Free, Dairy free, Nut free, Grain free, can be Soy free if soy free cream cheese is used

Ingredients:

8 oz non-dairy cream cheese
1 teaspoon onion powder
1 cup medium salsa
1/3 cup minced onions
1 cup chopped tomatoes
1 cup non-dairy cheddar cheese
2 tablespoons minced cilantro
2 cups lettuce thinly sliced

Directions:

1. Whip the cream cheese in a small bowl with a spoon until soft and spreadable. Add onion powder and mix well.
2. Layer all ingredients in an 8"x8" pan in this order: cream cheese, salsa, cheese, onions, tomatoes, cilantro and lettuce.
3. Serve with corn chips or fresh veggies.

CHANA SALAD SPREAD (EGGLESS EGG SALAD)

MAKES 2 CUPS

Soy Free, Gluten Free, Dairy Free, Nut Free, Grain Free

Ingredients:

1 can chickpeas
2 tablespoons onions, finely chopped
1/4 cup celery, minced
1/4 cup dill pickles, minced
1/3 cup non-dairy mayo
1/2 teaspoon sea salt
1/4 teaspoon black pepper
1/2 teaspoon mustard
1/2 teaspoon turmeric
Squeeze of a lemon

Directions:

1. Strain can of chickpeas then dry them in a paper towel to get them as dry as possible.
2. Mash the chickpeas enough to get rid of large pea pieces.
3. Add remaining ingredients and mix well. Let sit for 10 minutes before serving.
4. Serve as a sandwich, with crackers, chips or fresh vegetables.

BETTER THAN MOVIE POPCORN

SERVES 4 PEOPLE

Soy Free, Gluten Free,
Dairy Free, Nut Free

Ingredients:

1/2 cup organic popcorn

3-4 tablespoons non dairy margarine divided

3-4 tablespoon nutritional yeast

1-1 1/4 teaspoon sea salt or to taste

Directions:

1. Add Popcorn to an Air Popcorn Popper Machine

2. Put cover on and if there is a space to add the margarine, add 1 tablespoon for melting.

3. Place a large pot under the popper and add remaining margarine to pot in small pieces.

4. Turn the popper on and mix the margarine around the bowl to help it melt as the air is heating it.

5. As the popcorn is popping into the pot mix with margarine.

6. Once all popcorn is done add nutritional yeast and 1 teaspoon of salt. Mix well making sure all margarine in the pot is melted and evenly dispersed. Then add remaining melted margarine.

7. Taste and see if the remaining salt or nutritional yeast should be added.

SUMMER ROLLS

MAKES 10 ROLLS

Gluten Free, Dairy Free,
Nut Free, can be Soy Free

Ingredients:

For the tofu or chickpeas:
1 block of tofu or 2 cans chickpeas
2 garlic cloves, minced
1/4 cup onions, minced
2 tablespoons toasted sesame oil
1/2 teaspoon sea salt
1/4 cup low sodium vegetable broth
1 teaspoon agave
1 1/2 teaspoon freshly ground black pepper or to taste
1/4 cup oil

Veggies:

2 cups carrots, grated or julienne
4 cups lettuce, shredded
5 green onions, chopped
Fresh mint or basil, about 1-2 cups
10 rice paper wrappers

**I like to separate the veggies into equal piles for easier assembly and to make sure each roll gets enough filling. (see image A)

Directions:

1. Cut tofu into 1/2 inch strips (see page 16).
2. In plastic bag, combine all ingredients for the tofu or chickpeas except the oil.
   Marinate for about 20 minutes.
3. Heat a medium non-stick or cast iron pan on medium heat and add oil. Add tofu or chickpeas and brown both sides.
4. In a bowl of warm water, dip each rice paper wrapper, just enough to coat them. Do not over soak your wrapper! Place on your work surface and allow rice paper to soak up water and become gelatinous and pliable (about 10 seconds depending on the thickness of rice paper).
5. Lay veggies on the bottom third of wrapper closest to you. Then add tofu or chickpeas and herbs. Place enough herbs for every bite but do not over fill the roll or it will tear. [see image A]
6. Roll away from you about 1/3 of the way and push down as you roll. Pack the ingredients tight as you roll.
7. Fold in the sides into the center and continue to roll, packing the ingredients as you go to make a perfectly tight roll. [see image B]

Serve with sweet chili sauce (see page 166) or your favorite sweet and spicy sauce.

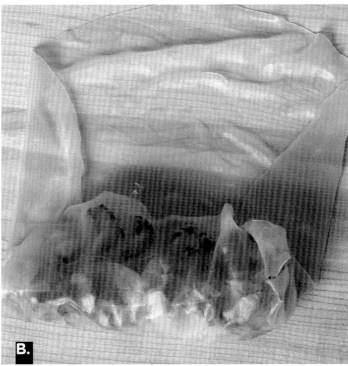

A.

B.

COLLARD GREEN ROLLS

MAKES 10-12 ROLLS

Soy Free, Gluten Free,
Dairy Free, Nut Free

Ingredients:

10-12 large collard greens
4 ounces of mei fun or vermicelli rice noodles
1/2 cup diced tomatoes
1/4 - 1/2 cup chickpeas, chopped
1 cup shredded carrots
1 cup thinly sliced, cabbage, bok choy or spinach
1/2 cup bell pepper, minced
2 green onions, minced
1 tablespoon sesame seeds

Sauce:

2 tablespoons toasted sesame oil
1 tablespoons rice vinegar
2 teaspoons lemon juice
2 tablespoons cilantro or basil, minced
1 1/2 teaspoon sea salt

Directions:

1. Cut bottom stems off collard greens.
2. In a pot of boiling lightly salted water, blanch the collard greens stem side down for one minute each. Set them gently on a towel to dry.
3. Prepare the noodles according to package directions. Drain the noodles and rinse with cold water to stop the cooking process.
4. Mix the sauce in a large bowl then add the noodles and the remaining ingredients and mix well.
5. To prepare wraps, lay out one collard leaf with the stem side towards the bottom. Place about 1/3-1/2 cup of the noodle mix at the bottom of the leaf. [see image A]
6. Fold the bottom of the leaf over the filling. Fold in each side of the collard green leaf and continue to fold up until you have a burrito-like wrap. [see image B]
7. Set aside and repeat the process with the rest of the wraps.

A.

B.

QUINOA BLACK BEAN SALAD

SERVES 3-4 PEOPLE

Soy Free, Gluten Free,
Dairy Free, Nut Free

Ingredients:

1 head of romaine or green leaf lettuce

1 cup chopped tomatoes

1 cup chopped cucumbers

1/4 cup minced onions

1 ripe avocado chopped

1 can black beans (red or chickpeas)

1/4 cup water

1/2 teaspoon chili powder

1/2 teaspoon granulated garlic or garlic powder

1 1/2 cups cooked quinoa

2 gluten free tortillas

Enough oil for frying

Optional additional veggies: shredded beets, shredded radishes, shredded carrots

Dressing Ingredients:

3 tablespoons mustard

3 tablespoons + 1 teaspoon agave

1/4 teaspoon sea salt

2 tablespoons olive or sesame oil

Pinch red pepper flakes

Directions:

1. In a small pot, bring 1 cup of water to a boil then add 1/2 cup dried quinoa, and a pinch of salt and pepper. Cover, reduce heat to low and cook for 20 minutes.

2. Drain beans and add to a small pot with 1/4 cup water, chili powder, garlic and a pinch of salt and pepper. Cook beans on medium-low heat until warm.

3. Mix dressing ingredients in a small bowl and sit to the side.

4. Heat a small frying pan and add enough oil for frying. Cut tortillas into 1/4 inch strips and fry in oil for about 30 seconds, or until lightly browned. Drain on paper towels

5. In a large bowl cut or tear lettuce, leave a hole in the middle and add cooked quinoa, and top with beans. Then top with tomatoes, cucumber, onions and avocados.

6. Add dressing and tortilla strips then serve.

ITALIAN HOT POCKET

MAKES 5- 6 WRAPS

Soy Free, Gluten Free,
Dairy Free, Nut Free

Ingredients:

2 cups Italian ground burger (see page 104)

3 cups Italian kale (see page 123)

Non-dairy cheddar cheese

5-6 Gluten free tortillas

Directions:

1. Prepare the Italian veggie burger and Italian kale recipes.

2. Heat a medium pan on medium-low heat. Warm a tortilla just enough to soften. Cover for 45 seconds to 1 minute. Repeat with each tortilla. After warming tortillas keep pan on.

3. Add about 2-3 tablespoons of non-dairy cheese on top of the warm tortilla. Add the veggie burger and kale on top just enough so that you can close tortilla.

4. Fold in both sides of the tortilla then roll it like a burrito.

5. Add a little oil to heated pan and place the wrap, folded side down in the pan. Brown on both sides. The tortilla should brown enough where it will stick together. Repeat for remaining wraps.

6. If wraps will not close after heating, cover each one in foil or plastic wrap.

KALE SALAD RAPS

MAKES 4-5 WRAPS

Soy Free, Gluten Free,
Dairy Free, Nut Free

Ingredients:

8 oz of pre seasoned Tempeh or Italian ground burger (see page 104)

3 cups kale salad (see page 123)

1 ripe avocado, peeled and sliced

1 cup sliced tomatoes

Non-dairy mayo

4-5 Gluten free tortillas

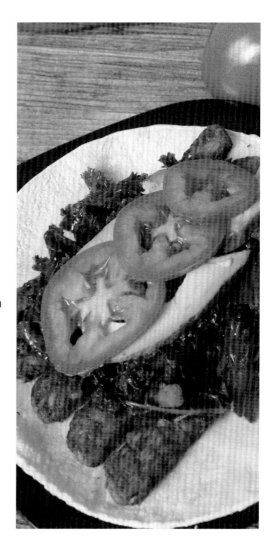

Directions:

1. Prepare the Italian veggie burger and kale recipes.
   If using tempeh, heat a medium sized pan on medium heat, add a little oil and brown tempeh on both sides. Remove from pan.
2. Warm a tortilla in a medium pan on medium-low heat just enough to soften. Cover for 45 seconds to 1 minute. Repeat with each tortilla. After warming tortillas keep pan on if doing step 5.
3. Spoon about 2 teaspoons of mayo on top of the warm tortilla. Add the veggie burger (or Tempeh), kale, tomatoes and sliced avocados on top, just enough so that you can close tortilla.
4. Fold in both sides of the tortilla then roll it like a burrito.
5. Optional Step: Add a little oil to heated pan and place the wrap, folded side down in the pan. Brown on both sides. The tortilla should brown enough where it will stick together. Repeat for remaining wraps.
6. If wraps do not fully close, wrap each one in plastic wrap or foil and serve.

REGGAE PATTIES

MAKES 9 PATTIES

Soy Free, Gluten Free,
Dairy Free

Crust:

2 1/4 cups all-purpose gluten free flour
1/2 teaspoon curry powder
1 teaspoon turmeric
1/2 teaspoon sea salt
1/2 cup non-dairy margarine, cold
1 tablespoon + 2 teaspoons agave
2 tablespoons coconut milk
2 teaspoons apple cider vinegar
1/4 cup + 3 tablespoons cold water

Filling:

1 tablespoon oil
1/2 cup onion, finely chopped
3 cloves garlic, minced
(about 1 tablespoon)
1/2 teaspoon grated ginger
2 cups thinly sliced cabbage
3/4 cup shredded carrots
1 cup broccoli, chopped small
1 teaspoon agave
1 cup low sodium vegetable broth

Spices:

2 teaspoons curry powder
1/4 teaspoons dried oregano
1/8 teaspoon dried thyme
1/8 teaspoon ground allspice
1 teaspoon sea salt

Directions:

To make crust:

1. Combine flour, curry powder, and salt in a food processor.
2. Add margarine and pulse until mixture resembles coarse meal.
3. Mix together agave, coconut milk and vinegar and add to dough. Pulse lightly.
4. Add cold water; process until dough forms. Dough should be slightly wet and sticky. Wrap in plastic wrap, and let sit for 30 minutes.

Preheat oven to 350°F

To make filling:

1. Heat oil in a medium skillet over medium heat. Add onion, garlic

and ginger and sauté 3 minutes. Add in cabbage, carrots and broccoli and sauté for 5 minutes.

2. Add in spices, agave and vegetable broth. Reduce heat to medium-low, and simmer 12-15 minutes and cook until most of the liquid has evaporated.

3. Lay parchment paper over a baking sheet or lightly coat baking sheet with oil.

4. Tear off two sheets of parchment paper large enough to roll out half of the dough. Sprinkle a little flour on one side of the parchment paper.

5. Grab half of the dough and sprinkle a little flour on it. Roll out dough to 1/8-inch thickness in between both sheets of parchment paper. Flipping over to make sure dough does not stick, you may need to add a little more flour.

6. Cut into 6-inch circles. [using a bowl, see image A] Place 1$^{1/2}$ tablespoons of filling in centers. [see image B] Fold circles in half, crimping edges with fork to seal. Use a spatula to remove patties from the parchment paper and place them on the prepared baking sheet.

7. Continue this process with remaining dough and filling. Bake for 12-15 minutes, bottoms will be golden brown.

SPLIT PEA CAKES

SERVES 4-6 PEOPLE

Soy Free, Gluten Free,
Dairy Free, Nut Free, Grain Free

Ingredients:

1 1/2 cups dried split peas

1 teaspoon sea salt or to taste

1/4-1/2 teaspoon red pepper flakes
or to taste

1/4-1/2 cup low sodium vegetable broth

Juice of 1/2 lemon

1/2 cup minced onions

1/2 cup minced fresh cilantro

Enough oil for frying

Directions:

1. Soak peas for a minimum of 3-4 hours to overnight then strain.

2. Blend split peas in a food processor with salt, red pepper flakes,
lemon juice and 1/4 cup vegetable broth until you get a smooth
paste. If it's not smooth enough, add another 1/4 cup of vegetable
broth.

3. Remove mixture from food processor and put into a bowl. Fold in
onions and cilantro.

4. Heat a small pan on medium-high heat and add enough oil for
frying. Spoon 1/4 cup of mixture into hot oil and fry on both sides
until golden brown. Do not overcrowd the pan; cook about 4 at a
time and strain on a paper towel.

COLLARD GREEN CHIPS

SERVES 4 PEOPLE

Soy Free, Gluten Free,
Dairy Free, Nut Free, Grain Free

Ingredients:

10 collard green leaves
2 teaspoons toasted sesame oil
2 teaspoons rice wine (mirin)
3 tablespoons nutritional yeast
1 teaspoon granulated garlic or garlic powder
1/2 teaspoon granulated onion or onion powder
1/2 teaspoon ground ginger
1/4 teaspoon sea salt or to taste

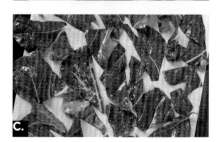

Directions:

1. Preheat oven to 300 degrees. Line 2 large baking sheets with parchment paper.
2. Wash greens, stack a few of similar size then cut around stems to remove it. [see image A]
3. Next cut leaves in a diagonal chip shape as much as possible. [see image B]
4. Put oil and mirin in a large bowl. Mix and rub greens with oil/mirin mixture making sure each leaf is covered.
5. Mix dry ingredients well in a small cup, then add the dry mixture a little at a time to greens making sure each leaf has some seasoning.
6. Lay chips in a single layer on parchment paper making sure there are none over lapping. [see image C]
7. Both sheets can be put into the stove at the same time in the middle of the oven.
8. Cook for 11 minutes then check for any that seem done or if edges are turning brown, remove those and continue to cook remaining for 2-3 more minutes.

SWEET POTATO PIZZA

MAKES 2 CUPS

Soy Free, Gluten Free,
Dairy Free, Nut Free

Dry Ingredients:

3/4 cup all purpose gluten free flour
1 teaspoon baking powder
1 1/4 teaspoon sea salt
1/2 teaspoon garlic powder
1 teaspoon coconut sugar

Wet Ingredients:

1 cup mashed sweet potato (about 1 medium)
2 1/4 teaspoon flax seed meal
1 1/2 tablespoons milk
2 teaspoons oil

Sauce Ingredients:

1 cup crushed tomatoes
1/4 teaspoon Italian seasoning
1/4 teaspoon basil
1/4 teaspoon oregano
1/4 teaspoon sea salt
1/4 teaspoon black pepper

Toppings:

Non-dairy cheese
Spinach
Onions
Bell peppers
Olives
Corn
Mushrooms

Directions:

Pre heat oven to 400 degrees

1. Boil the sweet potato in a small pot until soft. About 25 minutes.
2. Mix together the flax meal and milk and sit to the side.
3. Mix together the dry ingredients in a medium bowl.
4. Mix sauce ingredients in a small bowl or use your favorite pizza sauce.
5. Once potato is done let cool enough to peel then mash.
6. Using hand mix together dry mix and sweet potato a little at a time until well incorporated.
7. Add oil to flax mixture and add to dough and mix well. Then separate dough into two equal pieces
8. On a floured surface, roll the dough out to a rectangle and roll thin, (If the dough is difficult to roll, roll between layers of parchment paper.)
9. Brush dough with olive oil and flip onto a cookie sheet.
10. Repeat steps 8 and 9 with other crust.
11. Pre-bake crusts for 8-10 minutes.
12. Remove crusts from oven and brush with a thin layer of olive oil. Then add sauce, cheese and remaining toppings.
13. Cook pizzas for 12-15 minutes until crust begins to lightly brown.

BLUE NOTE BAKED NACHOS

SERVES 4 PEOPLE

Soy Free, Gluten Free,
Dairy Free, Nut Free

Ingredients:

8-10 ounces blue corn chips

1 can black beans

1 1/2 cup non-dairy cheddar cheese

Mango salsa (page 163)

Pico de gallo

Olives

Chopped tomatoes

Lettuce

Fresh spinach

Chopped onions

Cilantro

Bell peppers

Guacamole

Directions:

1. Preheat oven to 350 degrees. Lightly grease a 9x9 inch baking dish.
2. Place the black beans in a saucepan over medium heat. Add a pinch of salt and pepper and stir until thoroughly heated.
3. Layer half the chips, and 1/2 cup cheese, on the bottom of prepared baking dish. Spoon the beans over the chip mixture.
4. Add remaining chips and cheese and Bake in preheated oven until the cheese melts throughout, 15 to 18 minutes.
5. Top with remaining ingredients.

Jamaican
Curry Tofu
(pg 110)

clockwise from left:
**Curry Fela-fel (pg 105);
Spicy Singapore Noodles
(pg 107); Smokin' Potpie
(pg 108)**

*injera is a spongy Ethiopian bread made from teff that is used as the "fork" for eating. It can be found at your local Ethiopian restaurant or online.

clockwise from left:
Soprano Spaghetti (pg 103);
Ethiopian Platter (pg 109, 111, 126-129); Broccoli Casserole (pg 102)

THE VEGAN REMIX

HEADLINERS

MAIN SELECTIONS

bb king tofu

hey sloppy joes

shepherd's pie

broccoli casserole

soprano spaghetti

italian ground veggie burger

curry fela-fel

chana masala

spice singapore noodles

smokin' potpie

yekik alicha

jamaican curry tofu

miser wat

twerkin' tacos

BB KING TOFU

SERVES 4 PEOPLE

Gluten Free. Nut Free, Dairy Free, Grain Free, Can be Soy Free if using hemp tofu

Ingredients:

1/4 cup oil or enough for frying

One 15 ounce block extra firm tofu

Marinade for Tofu:

1 teaspoon granulated garlic or garlic powder

1 teaspoon chili powder

1 teaspoon onion powder

1/2 cup low sodium vegetable broth

Sauce:

1/2 cup ketchup

1 tablespoon molasses

2 teaspoon granulated garlic

1 teaspoon chili powder

1 teaspoon sea salt

1 teaspoon black pepper

1/2 teaspoon smoked paprika

1/2 cup water

Veggies:

1/2 cup onion, chopped

1/2 cup green pepper, chopped

3 cloves garlic chopped, about 1 1/2 teaspoon minced

Directions:

1. Cut tofu into steaks and add marinade. Let sit for a minimum of 30 minutes.
2. While tofu is marinating, add sauce ingredients to a small pot and simmer for 20 minutes stirring occasionally.
3. Heat a cast iron skillet or non-stick pan on medium heat. Add oil then immediately add tofu to minimize grease splattering.
4. Fry tofu on both sides until brown.
5. Add veggies and cook until soft.
6. Add sauce, cover and simmer for 15 min.

FRYING TOFU

HEY SLOPPY JOES

MAKES 4-6 WRAPS OR SANDWICHES

Soy Free, Gluten Free, Dairy Free, Nut Free

Ingredients:

2 tablespoons oil
10-12 ounces of veggie burger
or 1 1/2 cup dried mushrooms chopped
1/4 cup chopped onion
1/4 cup bell pepper, chopped
6 gluten free tortillas or hamburger buns

Spices:

1/2 teaspoon ground fennel seed
1 teaspoon smoked paprika
1 teaspoon garlic powder
1/2 teaspoon sea salt

Sauce:

1 cup canned crushed tomatoes
1/2 cup ketchup
1 teaspoon molasses
3 tablespoons agave
1 tablespoon mustard
2 teaspoons chili powder
2 teaspoons sea salt
1 teaspoon black pepper
1 teaspoon granulated garlic
or garlic powder
1/4 cup water

Directions:

1. If using dried mushrooms, soak in warm water for 10 minutes and strain. Keep liquid to use for other recipes.
2. Add sauce ingredients to a small pot and simmer on low for 10 minutes. Stirring occasionally.
3. Heat non-stick skillet on medium heat and add oil.
4. Add veggie burger patties and brown on both sides. After browned, break up burger with a spatula to make a crumble.
5. Spread crumble or mushrooms flat and cook for 2 minutes. Making sure most have browned, mix and lay flat again and cook for 2 more minutes.
6. Add spices and cook for 2 minutes, then add green pepper and onions and sauté until veggies are soft. Turn off.
7. Depending on the type of burger you use will determine how you use the sauce. If you are using soy based, wheat based burger or mushrooms, add the sauce and mix. Soy free and gluten free burgers can get soggy easily so instead of mixing the sauce in it, just top the crumble with 2-3 tablespoons of sauce once you put it in the tortilla or bun.
8. If you are using a tortilla, add crumble and sauce then fold in both sides of the tortilla then roll it like a burrito.
9. Add a little oil to heated pan and place the wrap folded side down in the pan. Brown on both sides. The tortilla should brown enough where it will stick together. Repeat for remaining wraps.
10. If wraps will not close after heating cover each one in foil or plastic wrap.

SHEPHERDS PIE

SERVES 4-6 PEOPLE

Soy Free, Gluten free,
Nut free, Dairy free

Ingredients:

1 cup brown or green lentils, dry
2 cups water
2 tablespoons of nutritional yeast (optional)

Ingredients for Potatoes:

6 medium potatoes
Enough water to cover potatoes
1/4 teaspoon sea salt
1/4 teaspoon black pepper
2 tablespoons non-dairy margarine or oil
1/2 cup unsweetened non-dairy milk

Sauce:

3 tablespoons non-dairy margarine or oil
2 tablespoons all-purpose gluten free flour
1 cup mushroom broth or low sodium vegetable broth
2 tablespoons tomato paste or sauce
3-4 sprigs fresh thyme, finely chopped or a pinch of dried
2 teaspoons sea salt
1 teaspoon black pepper
1 tablespoon toasted sesame oil

Veggies:

1 tablespoon oil
1/2 cup onion, finely diced
1/2 cup bell peppers, finely minced
1 teaspoon minced garlic
1 cup carrots, finely diced
1 cup frozen peas

Garnish:

1/4 cup chopped cilantro leaves
2 scallions, thinly sliced
Lime wedges and sliced chilies

Directions:

Preheat oven to 400°F degrees.

Potatoes:

1. Roughly cut potatoes, add to a pot, cover with water and bring to a boil. It's optional if you want to peel the potatoes, but I don't.
2. Boil for 15-20 minutes until soft.
3. Drain potatoes and return back to pot.
4. Mash the potatoes and then add salt, pepper, margarine and milk. Continue to mash until smooth.

Lentils:

1. While potatoes are boiling, bring 2 cups of water to a boil in a small pot.
2. Add the lentils and reduce heat to a medium-high and boil for 15 minutes.
3. In the last 5 minutes of cooking, lightly stir the lentils occasionally to make sure they don't stick.

Sauce:

**To reduce pot and pan usage you can wait until the lentils are done and use that same pot to make the sauce, or just start the sauce in another small pot.

1. Heat a small pot on medium-low and add the margarine and flour. Cook for 3-5 minutes, making sure it does not burn.
2. Slowly whisk in vegetable broth and make sure there are no lumps.
3. Add remaining ingredients simmer on low for 3-5 minutes until thick, stirring occasionally.

Veggies:

While potatoes, lentils and sauce are cooking, sauté veggies in a pan, with oil for 5 minutes or until soft.

Assemble:

Once everything is cooked, layer ingredients in a medium casserole dish putting the lentils on the bottom then the veggies.

Then pour the sauce over the veggies. Top with the mashed potatoes, starting around the edges to create a seal to prevent the mixture from bubbling up and smooth with a rubber spatula. Sprinkle nutritional yeast evenly on top of potatoes.

Place on a parchment lined half sheet pan on the middle rack of the oven and bake for 25 minutes, or just until the potatoes begin to brown. Remove and cool for at least 15 minutes before serving.

BROCCOLI CASSEROLE

SERVES 6-8 PEOPLE

Gluten Free, Nut Free,
Dairy Free, Can be Soy Free

Ingredients:

One 16 oz bag frozen broccoli

1 1/2 cup instant brown rice

1/2 cup onions, minced

1/2 cup celery, minced

2 cups cream of mushroom soup (see page 59)

2 cups unsweetened non-dairy milk

1 cup of shredded non-dairy cheddar cheese

1 block extra firm tofu or 1 can chickpeas

1/2 cup gluten free bread crumbs + 4 teaspoons oil (optional)

Spices:

1 teaspoon garlic powder

1 teaspoon onion powder

1/2 teaspoon black pepper

3 teaspoons sea salt or to taste

1/4 teaspoon dried thyme

1/4 teaspoon dried sage

2 tablespoons nutritional yeast

Protein Spices:

1/4 cup oil for tofu or 2 teaspoons oil
for chickpeas

1/2 teaspoon onion powder

1/2 teaspoon garlic powder

1/4 teaspoon sea salt

Directions:

1. Pre heat oven to 400°F degrees.
2. If using tofu, cut into steaks then heat a cast iron skillet or non-stick pan on medium heat, add oil then immediately add tofu to reduce oil splattering.
3. Brown tofu on first side, flip over, add protein spices and cook for a few more minutes, then remove from heat and drain.
4. If using chickpeas add with oil to a cast iron skillet or non-stick pan on medium heat, lightly brown then add spices. Do not over cook or chickpeas will dry out.
5. While protein is cooking, mix remaining ingredients, except breadcrumbs in a 9x13 inch casserole pan preferably with a lid, if not just cover with aluminum foil.
6. If using tofu cut into small cubes and mix in with remaining ingredients. If using chickpeas just layer on the top of mixed ingredients.
7. Mix breadcrumbs and oil and evenly sprinkle over the top.
8. Cover and bake 30 minutes then uncover and bake 15 more minutes.
9. Serve while hot.

SOPRANO SPAGHETTI

SERVES 6-8 PEOPLE

Soy Free, Gluten free,
Dairy free, Nut free

Ingredients:

16 oz pack of gluten free spaghetti noodles

3 tablespoons oil, divided

Veggies:

One 28 oz can whole or diced tomatoes

2 teaspoons minced garlic

1/2 cup onions, chopped

1/2 cup carrots, chopped

1/2 cup bell peppers, chopped

Spices:

1/2 teaspoon Italian seasoning

2 teaspoons dried basil

1 teaspoon dried oregano

1 teaspoon sea salt or to taste

1/2 teaspoon black pepper

1/4 teaspoon ground fennel seed

1 teaspoon agave

Garnish:

Top with nutritional yeast like parmesan cheese (optional)

Directions:

1. In a medium pot, sauté all veggies except tomatoes in 1 tablespoon oil on medium-low heat until soft. About 5 minutes.
2. Add spices and sauté for about 1 minute.
3. Add tomatoes and cover. Simmer 10 minutes stirring every couple of minutes, mashing tomatoes to break them up. Then uncover and simmer for 10 more minutes.
4. While sauce is simmering, cook noodles. I always check noodles 2-3 minutes before the package suggests it should be done since gluten free noodles can get mushy easy.
5. Strain noodles, rinse with cold water to stop the cooking process and add 2 tablespoons olive oil to reduce sticking. Then return back to the pot.
6. Put noodles in serving bowls and top with sauce and Italian veggie burger (see page 104).

ITALIAN GROUND VEGGIE BURGER

4-6 SERVINGS

Dairy free, Can be Soy free, Gluten free, Grain free and Nut free depending on the burger used.

Ingredients:

8-10 ounces veggie burger

3 tablespoons oil

2 tablespoons tomato sauce or ketchup

Veggies:

1/2 cup minced onion

2 cloves garlic, crushed

1/2 cup green bell pepper, minced

Spices:

1 teaspoon sea salt

1 teaspoon ground fennel

1 teaspoon Italian seasoning

1/2 teaspoon black pepper

1 teaspoon smoked paprika

2 teaspoons whole sage (optional)

Directions: *If using already ground burger skip to step 3

1. Heat a cast iron or non-stick skillet on a medium heat. Add oil and veggie burger.

2. If using veggie burger patties brown on both sides then break them into large pieces: Use a stiff spatula to break the burger into several pieces.

3. Break the burger into smaller pieces and brown. Continue breaking the burger into smaller and smaller pieces. Stir the burger occasionally to make sure it's browning evenly. Cook for about 5 minutes. Sprinkle with the spices and sauté for 2 more minutes.

4. Remove burger from pan and sit to the side.

5. Add veggies to the pan and sauté until lightly soft, about 3 minutes. Add burger back to the pan, then add the tomato sauce and sauté 2 more minutes.

CURRY FELA-FEL

SERVES 5-6 PEOPLE

Soy free, Gluten free,
Dairy free, Nut Free

Ingredients:

1 1/2 cup dried chickpeas
1/2 cup onion, chopped
1/4 cup fresh cilantro, chopped or 1 teaspoon dry
1/4 cup fresh parsley, chopped or 1 teaspoon dry
2 cloves garlic, minced (about 1 teaspoon)
6 gluten free tortillas or 6 whole grain pitas
Topping Options: chopped tomato, lettuce,
onions, radishes, cucumbers or spinach

Spices:

2 teaspoons ground cumin
1 teaspoon ground coriander
2 tablespoons yellow curry powder
1 1/2 teaspoon sea salt
2 teaspoons granulated garlic
1/2 teaspoon black pepper
1 teaspoon baking powder
1/2 cup chickpea flour
Juice of 1 lemon
Oil for frying

Dressing:

1/4 cup non-dairy mayo
1/2 cucumber, peeled and chopped
1 teaspoon minced garlic
1 teaspoon dried dill weed
1/4 cup tahini
1/2 teaspoon sea salt or to taste

1/2 teaspoon black pepper or to taste
1 teaspoon yellow curry powder (optional)
Juice of 1/2 lemon

Directions:

1. Soak peas overnight, then drain.
2. Pulse chickpeas in a food processor for about 15 seconds.
3. Add remaining ingredients and spices except for the dressing and mix into a paste. You may need to open food processor and help all ingredients get mixed evenly.
4. Remove from processor into a bowl, cover and let sit for 30 minutes.
5. While the falafel mix is sitting make the dressing.
6. Add all dressing ingredients to a blender and mix well.
7. Add to a small bowl, cover and refrigerate.
8. Heat a cast iron or non-stick pan on medium heat, then add enough oil to fry patties on both sides.
9. Shape about 2 tablespoons of the falafel mixture into patties.
10. Gently add patties to pan and fry on both sides until brown.
11. Remove patties from pan and drain on paper towels.
12. Add patties, toppings and dressing to either wrap or pita and enjoy!

CHANA MASALA

SERVES 4 PEOPLE

Soy Free, Gluten Free,
Dairy Free, Nut Free, Grain Free

Ingredients:

2 tablespoons oil

1 cup onions, minced

2 cloves garlic minced, about 2 teaspoons

1 tablespoon grated fresh ginger

2 cups diced canned tomatoes or 2 cups
 fresh tomatoes

1 can chickpeas

1 cup water

1 cup low sodium vegetable broth, divided

The juice of 1/2 lemon

1 tablespoon fresh cilantro

1 tablespoon non-dairy margarine (optional)

Spices:

1 teaspoon ground coriander

2 teaspoons ground cumin

1/2 teaspoon fennel seeds

2 cardamom pods

1 teaspoon garam masala

1 teaspoon sea salt

1 teaspoon amchoor (mango) powder

4 whole cloves

1 bay leaf

Directions:

1. Heat large skillet on medium-low heat and add oil.

2. Add onion, garlic and ginger, then sauté for 5 minutes.

3. Add tomatoes, cover and simmer on medium heat for 10 minutes stirring occasionally.
   Add a little vegetable broth if needed.

4. Add spices, cover and simmer for 3 minutes.

5. Add remaining ingredients, cover and simmer for 20 minutes.

6. Uncover and simmer for 5-10 more minutes, stirring occasionally.

Top with cilantro

SPICY SINGAPORE NOODLES

SERVES 4 PEOPLE

Gluten free, Dairy free, Nut free, can be Soy Free

Ingredients:

1/2 cup oil, divided

1/2 block extra firm tofu or 1 can chickpeas

16 ounces of mei fun or rice vermicelli noodles

Veggies:

1/2 cup dried shiitake mushrooms, soaked in 1 cup water

2 stalks celery, sliced thin

1/2 cup green bell pepper, chopped

1 medium yellow onion, chopped

2 medium carrots, sliced thin

6 water chestnuts, sliced thin

2 cups broccoli, chopped in bite sized pieces

Sauce:

1 tablespoon garlic, minced

1 tablespoon grated ginger

2 tablespoons yellow curry powder

1/2 teaspoon smoked paprika

2 1/2 teaspoons sea salt

1/2 teaspoon onion powder

1 teaspoon chili garlic sauce

1/2 cup mushroom broth or low sodium vegetable broth

2 tablespoons mirin (rice wine)

2 tablespoons toasted sesame oil

Garnish:

Peanuts or cashews

Lime

Chopped cilantro

Minced onions

Bean sprouts

Directions:

1. Soak mushrooms in warm water for half an hour. Drain, keeping liquid, then cut off the stems.

2. Slice the mushrooms thinly, and then heat a small pan on medium heat and sauté mushrooms in 1 tablespoon oil until brown.

3. Add 2 tablespoons of oil to the pan and add the curry powder, the ginger, and the minced garlic, and sauté until fragrant.

4. Add remaining sauce ingredients. Stir to combine and then cover and cook for 5 minutes. Remove pan from heat and set aside.

5. Put the noodles and broccoli in a large bowl and soak in enough hot water to cover, until the noodles are soft (about 4 to 6 minutes). Drain and set aside.

6. If using tofu, cut into cubes and pan fry in a large wok using 1/4 cup oil. Brown on all sides.

7. Add in the remaining vegetables and chickpeas (if using). Stir-fry for 3 minutes, until the vegetables start to soften.

8. Add in the noodles and broccoli to the vegetables.

9. Pour on the sauce and mix the ingredients thoroughly to coat all the noodles and incorporate all the vegetables

10. Top with garnish and serve hot.

SMOKIN' POTPIE

SERVES 4-6 PEOPLE

Soy Free, Gluten free,
Nut free, Dairy free

Ingredients:

2 gluten free piecrusts, frozen or fresh (see page 145)

Filling:

1 can chickpeas
1/2 cup onions, minced
1 cup frozen mixed veggies
1 cup potatoes, cubed small
2 tablespoons oil

Sauce:

1 tablespoon non-dairy margarine or oil
1 tablespoon all-purpose gluten free flour
1 tablespoon arrowroot or cornstarch
1/2 teaspoon dried thyme
1/2 teaspoon dried sage
1 teaspoon sea salt or to taste
1/2 teaspoon black pepper
1/2 cup low sodium vegetable broth
3/4 cup + 2 tablespoons of unsweetened non-dairy milk

Directions:

1. Pre heat oven to 400°F degrees.
2. Sauté potatoes in oil and cover for 10 minutes, stirring occasionally. You may need to add 1/4 cup of water to pan to stop from sticking.
3. Add onions, chickpeas and frozen veggies and sauté for 5-8 minutes. Remove from heat as soon as they soften lightly.
4. In a small pot melt margarine on medium-low heat.
5. Add flour and arrowroot, mix well.
6. Whisk in milk, broth and remaining sauce ingredients.
7. Stir sauce, cooking until it lightly bubbles and thickens. Turn off.
8. Lay one crust in bottom of 8 inch pie pan. Add veggies then pour sauce evenly on top.
9. Lay second crust on top and secure around the sides with fork or finger. Poke a few holes in the top of the crust with a fork.
10. Sit on baking sheet and bake for 20-25 minutes until crust is light brown.

YEKIK ALICHA
(ETHIOPIAN YELLOW SPLIT PEAS)

SERVES 4-6 PEOPLE

Soy free, Gluten free, Dairy free, Nut free, Grain free

Ingredients:

1 cup yellow split peas
5 cups water, divided
1 tablespoon oil
1/2 teaspoon turmeric
11/2 teaspoon sea salt

Veggies:

1 cup onion, minced
3-4 cloves garlic or 11/2 teaspoon minced
1 teaspoon fresh ginger, grated
2 slices of jalapeño pepper, seeds removed

Directions:

1. Bring 3 cups of water to a boil in a medium pot, then add the split peas. Boil on medium-high for 20 minutes, stirring occasionally.
2. While peas are boiling sauté onion, garlic and ginger in oil in a separate pan for 3-5 minutes until soft.
3. After 20 minutes add the sautéed veggies, turmeric and 2 cups of water to the peas.
4. Reduce to medium-low heat, add jalepenos and simmer for 30 more minutes, stirring occasionally.
5. Add salt at the end. May need to simmer beans a little longer for desired consistency.

JAMAICAN CURRY TOFU

SERVES 4 PEOPLE

Gluten Free, Dairy free, Grain free, can be Soy free if tofu is removed or if hemp tofu is used

Ingredients:

1 block extra firm tofu
Oil for frying (about 1/2 cup)

Veggies:

1 large carrot, chopped (about 1 1/2 cups)
1 cup onions, chopped
1 cup bell pepper, chopped
1 clove garlic minced, about 2 teaspoons
1 tablespoon grated ginger
1 can chickpeas (optional)
2 medium potatoes, about 1 1/2 cups

Spices:

3 tablespoons yellow curry powder
4-5 sprigs fresh thyme
1 whole scotch bonnet pepper
1 teaspoon granulated garlic or garlic powder
1 teaspoon granulated onion or onion powder
2 teaspoons turmeric
2 teaspoons sea salt

Sauce:

2 cups water
2 cups low sodium vegetable broth
Juice of 1/2 lime or lemon
1/4 cup coconut milk
2 tablespoons ketchup

Directions:

1. Cut tofu into steaks.
2. Using a medium non-stick pan, heat pan first, then add oil and tofu at the same time to reduce splattering of the oil.
3. Fry tofu, browning both sides.
4. Remove tofu from pan and drain on paper towels. Once it slightly cools, cut tofu into triangles or cubes.
5. Add all veggies except potatoes and chickpeas to the same pan and sauté 5 minutes. (If not using tofu add 1/4 cup oil to sauté veggies)
6. Add spices and cook 2 more minutes.
7. Add potatoes, chickpeas, tofu and sauce ingredients, bring sauce to a light boil on medium heat.
8. Turn down heat to medium-low, cover and simmer for 20 minutes.

MISER WAT
(ETHIOPIAN SPICED LENTILS)

SERVES 4-6 PEOPLE

Soy Free, Gluten Free,
Dairy free, Nut Free, Grain free

Ingredients:

1 cup green lentils

4-6 cups water

2 medium potatoes, cubed, roughly 2 cups

1 to 5 slices of jalapeño (cut in 1/4 inch slices)

Veggies:

1/4 cup oil

1 cup onion, minced

1 teaspoon grated ginger

1/2 cup green bell pepper, minced

3 cloves garlic, minced

1/4 cup canned crushed tomatoes or tomato sauce

Spices:

11/4 tablespoons berbere (see page 165)

2 teaspoons sea salt

1 teaspoon garam masala

1 teaspoon paprika

Juice of 1/4 lemon

1/4 teaspoon ground cayenne pepper (optional)

Directions:

1. Rinse lentils for 1-2 minutes or until water drains clear.

2. In a medium skillet, sauté all veggies, except tomatoes in oil for about 2-3 minutes.

3. Add tomatoes, cover and cook 10-12 minutes, stirring occasionally to reduce sticking. You may need to add a little water as well to reduce sticking.

4. Add spices, except salt and lemon, and cook for about 2 minutes. Depending on how spicy your berbere is and how spicy you want your lentils, you can add extra cayenne.

5. Add lentils, potatoes and jalapeños and 4 cups of water and bring to a boil.

6. Cook on medium-high heat for 20-25 minutes. Add 1-2 more cups of water if the lentils need further softening or to add more liquid to the sauce.

7. Add salt and lemon at the end.

TWERKIN TACOS

SERVES 4-6 PEOPLE

Gluten free, Dairy free, Nut free, can be Soy free depending on the type of burger used

Ingredients:
12-16 ounces of veggie burger
1/4 cup oil, divided

Veggies:
1/4 cup onion, diced
1/4 cup green pepper, diced
2 cloves garlic, diced

Spices:
1 tablespoon chili powder
1 tablespoon granulated onion or onion powder
1 tablespoon granulated garlic or garlic powder
1/2 teaspoon ground coriander
1/2 teaspoon ground cumin
1/2 teaspoon whole fennel seeds
1 1/2 teaspoon sea salt
1/2 teaspoon ground ancho chili
1 teaspoon smoked paprika
2 tablespoons tomato sauce

Shell Options:
Hard shell blue or yellow corn tacos
Soft shell corn tortillas
Gluten free tortillas
Corn Chips

Directions:
If using veggie burger patties follow steps 1 and 2.

1. Heat a non-stick pan on medium heat then add oil.
2. Lightly brown veggie burger on both sides then break up into ground burger with a spatula.

If using already ground burger add to pan with oil and brown for 2 minutes.

3. Continue to brown burger and lay flat evenly on pan for 2 minutes. Mix burger and repeat until burger is lightly brown.
4. Add veggies and sauté for 3 minutes. Add spices and sauté for 2 more minutes.
5. Add tomato sauce and sauté 2 more minutes.
6. If burger gets too crunchy add 2 tablespoons of water.
7. Add to your favorite shell and garnish with your favorite toppings.

Serve With:
Refried beans
Rice
Lettuce
Fresh spinach
Diced tomatoes
Minced onions

Chopped cilantro
Non-dairy cheese
Olives
Pico de gallo
Salsa
Mango salsa (see page 163)

Thai Fried
Quinoa
(pg 130)

clockwise from top left:
Gai lan (pg 124); Crispy
Fried Brussel Sprouts (pg
122); Garlic Green Beans
(pg 120)

BBQ Tofu Meal. Top (clockwise):
Fried Corn (pg 118);
Sauteed Cabbage (pg 119);
Maple Pan Yams (pg 118);
BBQ Tofu (pg 98)

Indian Meal. Top (clockwise):
Aloo Gobi (pg 125);
Coconut Yellow Rice (pg 131); Chana Masala (pg 106)

THE VEGAN REMIX

HIT SINGLES
SOULFUL SIDES

fried corn

maple pan yams

sautéed cabbage

sautéed broccoli

garlic green beans

scalloped potatoes

crispy fried brussel sprouts

italian kale

kale salad

gai lan (chinese broccoli)

aloo gobi (indian potatoes and cauliflower)

atalkilt wat (ethiopian cabbage)

gomen (ethiopian collard greens)

fosolia (ethiopian greenbeans)

mushroom tibs

thai fried quinoa

coconut yellow rice

beet and potato salad

cinnamon rice

FRIED CORN

SERVES 4-6 PEOPLE

Soy Free, Gluten Free,
Nut Free, Dairy Free

Ingredients:

3 tablespoons non-dairy margarine
1 cup onion, chopped
1 cup medium green bell peppers, chopped
1 teaspoon minced garlic
1 (16 ounce) package frozen corn
or 4 cups of fresh corn cut off the cob
1/2 teaspoon black pepper
1 teaspoon sea salt
1/2 cup low sodium vegetable broth

Directions:

1. Heat a medium pan on medium-low heat and add margarine.
2. Sauté onions, peppers and garlic for 3 minutes or until soft.
3. Add corn and remaining spices then increase heat to medium.
4. Cook for 10 minutes uncovered.

MAPLE PAN YAMS

SERVES 4-6 PEOPLE

Soy Free, Gluten Free,
Dairy Free, Nut Free, Grain Free

Ingredients:

2 1/2 lbs sweet potatoes, about 4-5 medium
1/2 cup water
2 tablespoons coconut oil or non dairy margarine

Spices:

3 tablespoons maple syrup
1 teaspoon molasses
1 teaspoon cinnamon
1 teaspoon nutmeg
1 teaspoon chili powder

Directions:

1. Cut yams into 1/2 inch thick rounds and layer in a pan.
2. Mix spices, oil and water in a small cup or bowl, then pour over the yams.
3. Heat pan on a medium heat, cover and simmer until soft. Cooking time is about 20-25 minutes.

SAUTEED CABBAGE

SERVES 4 PEOPLE

Soy Free, Gluten Free,
Dairy Free, Nut Free, Grain Free

Ingredients:

2 tablespoons oil

3/4 head of cabbage, thinly sliced

1/2 cup onions, thinly sliced

1/2 cup shredded carrots

1/2 cup green pepper, thinly sliced

2 tablespoons chopped celery

Spices:

1 teaspoon granulated garlic or garlic powder

1 teaspoon granulated onion or onion powder

1/2 teaspoon ground cumin

1/2 teaspoon dry basil

1/2 teaspoon oregano

1 teaspoon sea salt

1/2 teaspoon pepper or to taste

1 cup low sodium vegetable broth

Directions:

1. Slice cabbage into thin strips.

2. Heat a medium wok or pan on medium-low, add oil and all veggies except cabbage.

3. Sauté for 3 minutes then add cabbage and all spices except vegetable broth.
   Cover and cook for 5 minutes.

4. Uncover and mix vegetables well. Add broth, cover and cook 15 more minutes, mixing
   every 5 minutes.

SAUTEED BROCCOLI

SERVES 4 PEOPLE

Soy Free, Gluten Free,
Dairy Free, Nut Free, Grain Free

Ingredients:

1 pound broccoli, rinsed and trimmed

3 tablespoons oil

1 tablespoon minced garlic

1/4 cup onions, chopped

1/4 cup low sodium vegetable broth

1 teaspoon sea salt

1/2 teaspoon freshly ground black pepper

2 tablespoons nutritional yeast (optional)

Directions:

1. Heat a medium sized wok or pan on medium-low heat then add oil.
2. Add onion and garlic and sauté 3-5 minutes, making sure not to burn the garlic.
3. Add broccoli, salt, pepper and veggie broth. Cover on medium heat for 5 minutes.
4. Uncover and sprinkle on nutritional yeast. Mix well. Cook for 2-3 more minutes if you'd like until desired consistency. Serve hot.

GARLIC GREEN BEANS

SERVES 4-6 PEOPLE

Soy Free, Gluten Free,
Dairy Free, Nut Free, Grain Free

Ingredients:

1 lb green beans

2 tablespoons oil

3 tablespoons minced garlic

2 teaspoons sea salt or to taste

Directions:

1. Blanch green beans by letting them sit in boiling water for 2 minutes then strain.
2. Heat a medium wok or pan on low and add garlic. Sauté garlic on low for 5 minutes to immerse the oil with the garlic flavor. Making sure garlic does not burn.
3. Add green beans and salt then turn up heat to medium-high.
4. Stir fry beans for 5 minutes constantly mixing so garlic does not burn.
5. Turn heat off and cover for three minutes. Serve.

SCALLOPED POTATOES

SERVES 4-6 PEOPLE

Soy Free, Gluten Free,
Dairy Free, Nut Free, Grain Free

Ingredients:

4-5 large potatoes, cut in 1/4 inch slices
1/2 of one whole bell pepper, cut in thin slices
1 small onion, cut into thin slices
3/4 cup non-dairy cheddar cheese

Sauce:

1 cup unsweetened non dairy milk
2 tablespoons oil
1 teaspoon granulated onion
or onion powder
2 teaspoon granulated garlic
or garlic powder
1 teaspoon sea salt
1/2 teaspoon black pepper
1/4 cup low sodium vegetable broth
1/4 cup nutritional yeast

Directions:

1. Pre-heat oven to 450 degrees.

2. Layer potatoes, bell peppers and onions in a medium casserole pan, making the last layer potatoes.

3. In a small bowl mix the sauce ingredients then pour over the potatoes.

4. Spread the cheese evenly on top and cover.

5. Bake for 40 minutes until the potatoes are soft when a fork is poked through.

CRISPY FRIED BRUSSEL SPROUTS

SERVES 4-6 PEOPLE

Soy Free, Gluten Free,
Dairy Free, Nut Free, Grain Free

Ingredients:

1 lb brussel sprouts halved or quartered
Oil for frying

Serve with Sweet Chilli Sauce (page 166)

Directions:

1. In a large wok, deep pot or dutch oven, fill oil to about two inches high. Heat the oil to about medium-high heat. Test the oil by frying one piece of brussel sprouts first. If it sizzles and cooks quickly, then the oil is ready.***
2. Fry the brussel sprouts in batches, so start by frying about 1/4 of the sprouts until they are golden brown. Remove them from oil and blot them on paper towels to remove excess oil. Repeat the frying for the rest of the sprouts.
3. Once all brussel sprouts are fried and crispy, combine them in a large bowl. Toss the crispy sprouts with 2 to 3 tablespoons of the sweet chili sauce and serve warm.

**You might have some left over chili sauce, but that's ok. Save it for your next batch of fried brussel sprouts, spring rolls, french fries or even as a sauce for fried tofu. It will keep up to 7 days in refrigerator.

***Depending on your size of brussel sprouts cut them to appropriate bite-sized pieces. If your brussel sprouts are small, cut them in half. If they are very large, cut them in quarters. However you decide to cut them, make sure they're all about the same size so that they can cook evenly in the hot oil.

ITALIAN KALE

SERVES 4 PEOPLE

Soy Free, Gluten Free,
Dairy Free, Nut Free, Grain Free

Ingredients:

1 lb kale, coarsely chopped

3 tablespoons oil

2 cloves garlic, minced

2 cups tomatoes, diced

1 cup low sodium vegetable broth or water

1 teaspoon rice vinegar

Spices:

1 1/2 teaspoon smoked paprika

1/2 teaspoon black pepper

1 teaspoon sea salt

Directions:

1. Heat a large saucepan over medium-low heat then add oil.
2. Add the garlic and cook until soft, but not brown. Add tomatoes, cover and raise heat to medium.
3. Cook for 5-8 minutes on medium stirring occasionally. May need to add a little of the vegetable broth to stop sticking.
4. Add spices and lightly mash tomatoes to make a paste.
5. Add the broth, vinegar and kale and toss to combine. Cover and cook for 5 minutes. Remove cover and continue to cook for 2-3 more minutes.
6. Add more salt and pepper if necessary.

KALE SALAD

SERVES 4 PEOPLE

Soy Free, Gluten Free,
Dairy Free, Nut Free, Grain Free

Ingredients:

4 sun-dried tomatoes

1/4 cup warm water

1 lb of green kale

2 1/2 tablespoons toasted sesame oil

1/4 cup olive oil

3 teaspoons granulated garlic

1 1/2 -2 teaspoons sea salt

1/4 cup nutritional yeast

The juice of 1/2 lemon or lime

Directions:

1. Soak tomatoes in warm water and let sit for 20 minutes until soft.
2. Wash kale and cut in thin strips.
3. Mix oils, spices (1 1/2 teaspoon of salt), nutritional yeast and lemon juice in a medium bowl.
4. Cut tomatoes into thin strips or pieces. Add tomatoes and soaking water to oil mixture.
5. Add a little kale at a time and massage kale, about 2 minutes, to fully incorporate flavors and wilt kale.
6. Cover and let marinate for a minimum of 15 minutes. After it sits see if it needs more salt and add remaining.

GAI LAN (CHINESE BROCCOLI)

SERVES 4 PEOPLE

Soy Free, Gluten Free,
Dairy Free, Nut Free

Ingredients:

1 lb of Chinese broccoli (Gai Lan)
or collard greens
1½ tablespoons oil
5 whole garlic cloves, peeled and gently
smashed but left intact
1 inch of fresh ginger, sliced

Sauce:

1/4 cup low sodium vegetable broth
1 tablespoon Chinese rice wine (mirin)
1/4 teaspoon agave
2 tablespoons toasted sesame oil
1 teaspoon sea salt
1/4 teaspoon red pepper flakes

Directions:

1. Wash the gai lan and trim 1-inch from the ends of stalk and discard.
2. In large wok or pan (large enough to hold all stalks), heat just 1 tablespoon of the cooking oil over medium-low heat. When the oil is just starting to get hot (the garlic should sizzle upon contact) add the whole garlic cloves and let them fry until golden brown on all sides. Be careful not to burn the garlic, you just want to toast them - if the garlic starts turning dark brown, turn the heat to low. Toasting the garlic should take about 2 minutes.
3. While the garlic is toasting, mix the sauce ingredients in a small bowl and set aside.
4. Turn the heat to high and add the ginger, fry for 30 seconds. Add the gai lan stalks and use your spatula to scoop up the oil so that every stalk has been bathed with the ginger/garlic-infused oil for 30 seconds.
5. Pour the sauce mixture into the wok and immediately cover the wok with a tight fitting lid. Turn the heat to medium and let the vegetable steam for 3-4 minutes, until stalks can be easily pierced with a paring knife or fork.
6. Serve immediately. Keep in mind the stalks are meant to be eaten.

ALOO GOBI

SERVES 4 PEOPLE

Soy Free, Gluten Free,
Dairy Free, Nut Free, Grain Free

Ingredients:

2 tablespoons oil
2 teaspoons grated ginger
2 teaspoons garlic, minced
2 teaspoons jalapeños, chopped (seeds removed unless you want it spicy)
1 small head cauliflower, cut into small florets, about 3 cups
2 medium red or yellow potatoes cut into 1/2-inch cubes (similar size to cauliflower) about 2 cups
2 cups low sodium vegetable broth, divided
Juice of 1/2 a lemon

Spices:

1/2 teaspoon ground cumin
4 whole cardamom pods or 3/4 teaspoon ground
1 teaspoon turmeric
1 teaspoon garam masala
1 1/2 teaspoon sea salt

Garnish:

2 tablespoons freshly minced cilantro leaves

Directions:

1. Heat a medium pan or wok on medium-low heat. Add oil then sauté garlic, and ginger for 3 minutes.
2. Add spices and jalapeño then sauté 30 seconds. Then add 1/2 cup vegetable broth. Cook until the paste thickens and deepens in color slightly, about 3 minutes.
3. Add the cauliflower and potatoes, stirring to coat the vegetables with the spices.
4. Increase heat to medium. Add remaining vegetable broth and cover. Cook over medium heat 15 minutes. Then, remove the lid, stir, and cook until the cauliflower and potatoes are cooked through, about 5 minutes. Garnish with cilantro and serve.

SOULFUL SIDES

ATAKILT WAT (ETHIOPIAN CABBAGE)

SERVES 4 PEOPLE

Soy Free, Gluten Free,
Dairy Free, Nut Free, Grain Free

Ingredients:
2 large sweet potatoes cut into 1-inch cubes
3 carrots, sliced in large strips
1 cup onions, chopped
1/2 teaspoon grated ginger
2 teaspoons minced garlic
4 medium potatoes cut in large strips
(about 2 cups)
1/2 head cabbage, thinly sliced
1/2-1 cup vegetable broth or water

Spices:
1 teaspoon turmeric
1 teaspoon ground cumin
1/2 teaspoon black pepper
1/4 teaspoon berbere (see page 165)
1 1/2 teaspoon sea salt

Directions:
1. Heat a large pan over medium heat and add oil.
2. Add onion and cook for 3 minutes or until softened.
3. Add the potatoes, carrots, ginger, and garlic. Cover and cook for 8 minutes. Stirring every 3-4 minutes to prevent sticking.
4. Add the spices and sauté for 1 minute.
5. Stir in the cabbage and 1/2 cup of vegetable broth.
6. Reduce heat to medium-low, cover and let simmer for 10-15 minutes stirring occasionally.
7. If after 10 minutes cabbage is still not done and it's sticking, add remaining 1/2 cup of vegetable broth.

GOMEN
(ETHIOPIAN COLLARD GREENS)

SERVES 4-6 PEOPLE

Soy Free, Gluten Free,
Dairy Free, Nut Free, Grain Free

Ingredients:
1/3 cup oil
1 lb collard greens
1 cup low sodium vegetable broth
1 cup water

Veggies:
1 cup onions
4 teaspoons minced garlic
1 inch grated ginger
1 cup bell peppers, chopped
1 cup tomatoes, chopped

Spices:
1 1/2 teaspoons sea salt
1/4 teaspoon ground fenugreek
1 teaspoon ground cardamom or 1 whole cardamom pod
1/2 teaspoon ground cumin
1/4 teaspoon ground allspice
2-3 slices of jalapeño, seeds removed

Directions:
1. Heat a pan on medium-low heat then add oil and all veggies, except tomatoes.
2. Sauté vegetables for 2 minutes then add tomatoes, cover and sauté for 15 minutes on medium-high.
3. Check every 5 minutes and add a little broth at a time and stir to prevent sticking.
4. Add spices and cook for about 2 minutes.
5. Add the greens, water and any remaining vegetable broth to pot and simmer for 20 minutes, toss periodically.

FOSOLIA
(ETHIOPIAN GREEN BEANS)

SERVES 4-6 PEOPLE

Soy Free, Gluten Free,
Dairy Free, Nut Free, Grain Free

Ingredients:

1/4 cup oil

1 cup onion, chopped

1/2 cup green bell pepper, chopped

1 tablespoon ginger, grated

2 cloves of garlic, chopped or 1 tablespoon minced

1 cup tomato, chopped

3 large carrots, chopped

1 lb green beans

1 cup low sodium vegetable broth divided

1 tablespoon lemon juice

Spices:

1 teaspoon berbere (see page 165)

1/2 teaspoon coriander

1 1/2 teaspoon salt

1/4 teaspoon black pepper

Directions:

1. Heat a medium pan or wok on medium heat and add the oil.

2. Add the onions, peppers, ginger, garlic and tomatoes. Cover and cook for 10 minutes stirring occasionally. May need to add a little broth so it does not burn.

3. Add spices and mix for a minute then add carrots, green beans, veggie broth and lemon juice.

4. Cover and cook for 15- 20 minutes stirring occasionally.

MUSHROOM TIBS

SERVES 4 PEOPLE

Soy Free, Gluten Free,
Dairy Free, Nut Free, Grain Free

Ingredients:

3 tablespoons oil, divided

1 cup green bell pepper, cut into strips

1 large red onion, cut into strips

8 oz button mushrooms, cleaned and cut in 1/2 inch slices

Spices:

1/2 teaspoons granulated garlic or garlic powder

1/2 teaspoon smoked paprika

1 tablespoon + 1 teaspoon berbere (see page 165)

1/2 teaspoon sea salt

Directions:

1. Pour 2 tablespoons of oil over mushrooms and mix well making sure each is coated.

2. Mix spices together in a small bowl then pour over mushrooms and mix until each mushroom is covered.

3. Heat a medium cast iron skillet on medium-high heat. Add mushrooms and pan fry until lightly browned.

4. Remove mushrooms from pan and add 1 tablespoon of oil and sauté onions and peppers until lightly soft.

5. Turn heat off and add mushrooms and lightly toss.

THAI FRIED QUINOA

SERVES 4-6 PEOPLE
Soy Free, Gluten Free,
Dairy Free, Nut Free

Ingredients:

3 cups cold cooked quinoa preferably a day old
(1 cup dry equals 3 cups cooked)

Sauce:

1 tablespoon+ 1 teaspoon Thai red curry paste
2 tablespoon toasted sesame oil
2 tablespoons water
1 1/4 teaspoon sea salt
1/2 teaspoon chili garlic sauce
(optional depending on how spicy you like it)

Veggies:

1 tablespoon oil
1 1/4 cup small onion, diced
1/4 cup small bell pepper, diced
1 teaspoon minced garlic
1 cup frozen mixed veggies

Garnish:

Lightly chopped cilantro, mint or Thai basil for garnish
2 tablespoons roasted crushed peanuts (optional)

Directions:

1. In a small bowl, whisk the sauce ingredients together until they form a paste. Set aside.
2. Heat oil in a wok. Add onion and sauté until translucent. Then add the garlic, mixed veggies and bell pepper, and sauté for about 3 minutes.
3. Add the sauce and stir on high heat for about 30 seconds.
4. Add the cooked quinoa to the wok. Using a wide spatula, gently and quickly stir the quinoa to incorporate everything. Stir fry for about 2-3 minutes.
5. Top with crushed peanuts, chopped cilantro, mint or Thai basil.

COCONUT YELLOW RICE

SERVES 4 PEOPLE

Soy Free, Gluten Free,
Dairy Free

Ingredients:

1 1/2 cups long grain brown rice (jasmine or basmati)

1/8 teaspoon baking soda

1 can coconut milk

1 1/2 cups water

1 teaspoon turmeric

1 teaspoon sea salt

2 1/2 tablespoons unsweetened shredded coconut

Directions:

1. Soak rice in water with baking soda for a minimum of 5 minutes. Rinse and strain.

2. Add all ingredients except salt and shredded coconut to a medium pot. Stir and set over high heat. Bring to a bubbling (but not rolling) boil.

3. Immediately reduce heat to low and cover tightly with a lid.

4. Allow to cook for 35 minutes or until the coconut-water has been absorbed by the rice.

5. When all (or nearly all) of the coconut and water is gone, turn off the heat, but leave the pot on the burner (covered). Allow the rice to sit for another 5-10 minutes, or until you're ready to eat.

6. Add salt and shredded coconut then fluff the rice with chopsticks or a fork.

BEET AND POTATO SALAD

SERVES 4-5 PEOPLE

Soy Free, Gluten Free,
Dairy Free, Nut Free, Grain Free

Ingredients:

2 cups beets, cut in small cubes
1 cup potatoes, cut in small cubes
1/2 cup onion, minced
1/2 jalapeño, seeded and minced
2 tablespoons olive oil
Juice of 1 lemon
1/2 teaspoon sea salt or to taste

Directions:

1. Soak beets in water for 5 minutes then peel with a vegetable peeler.
2. Cut beets into small cubes and boil in a medium pot for 20 minutes or until soft.
3. Cut potatoes into small cubes and boil in a seperate small pot for 20 minutes or until soft
4. In a medium boil mix the remaining ingredients.
5. Strain potatoes then add to bowl, strain beets then add to bowl.
6. Toss ingredients. Serve warm or cold.

CINNAMON RICE

SERVES 3-4 PEOPLE

Soy Free, Gluten Free,
Dairy Free, Nut Free

Ingredients:

1 cup long grain brown rice (basmati or jasmine)
1/8 teaspoon baking soda
2 cups water
2 bay leaves
2 cardamom pods
4 whole cloves
1 inch cinnamon stick
1/4 teaspoon ground cumin
3/4 teaspoon sea salt
1 tablespoon non-dairy margarine
or coconut oil
1 tablespoon cilantro

Directions:

1. Soak rice in water with baking soda for a minimum of 5 minutes. Rinse and strain.
2. Bring 2 cups of water to a boil and add all ingredients except salt, margarine and cilantro.
3. Turn heat down to medium-low, cover cook for 35-40 minutes.
4. Let sit for 5 minutes covered, then add salt and margarine and mix well.

Garnish with cilantro

Mango Lassi
Popsicles
(pg 144)

clockwise from top left:
**Ice Cream Burgers
(pg 151); Smashing
Pumpkins Muffins
(pg 150); Sweet Potato
Pie (pg 143): Chocolate
Chip Cookies (pg 138)**

clockwise from top left:
Peanut Butter Cookies (pg 139); Strawberry Waffle Shortcake (pg 146); Georgia Peach Pie (pg 152): 5 Spice Rice Krispy Treats (pg 148)

THE VEGAN REMIX

SWEET NOTES
DESSERTS

CHOCOLATE CHIP COOKIES

YIELDS 3 DOZEN

Soy Free, Gluten Free, Dairy Free, Nut Free

Wet Ingredients:

1 cup sucanat

3/4 cup non-dairy margarine

1 tablespoon vanilla

1/2 cup maple syrup

Dry Ingredients:

2 1/4 cups all-purpose gluten free flour

1 teaspoon baking soda

1 teaspoon baking powder

2 tablespoons flax seed meal

1/4 teaspoon sea salt

3/4 cup mini or 1 1/4 cup regular size chocolate or carob chips

1/2 cup chopped walnuts or pecans (optional)

Directions:

1. Sit margarine out to soften.

2. In a large bowl, cream margarine by mixing with a spoon. Add sucanat and mix well.

3. Add vanilla and maple syrup. Mix well.

4. In a separate bowl, mix the dry ingredients.

5. Add dry ingredients into wet a third at a time and mix well.

6. Cover with plastic wrap and refrigerate for at least 30 minutes.

7. Preheat oven to 350°F and lightly grease a cookie sheet or cover with parchment paper.

8. Spoon dough onto sheet a tablespoon at a time.

9. Bake for 10-12 minutes, the bottoms should be golden brown.

Keep in mind that they continue to cook while on the pan. If they seem over cooked, bake for less time.

PEANUT BUTTER COOKIES

YIELDS 2 DOZEN

Soy Free, Gluten Free,
Dairy Free

Wet Ingredients:

1/2 cup non-dairy margarine

3/4 cup peanut butter, unsweetened and unsalted

1 1/2 cup sucanat

1 teaspoon vanilla extract

1/2 cup maple syrup

Dry Ingredients:

1 3/4 cup all-purpose gluten free flour

1 teaspoon baking soda

2 teaspoons baking powder

2 tablespoons flax seed meal

1/4 teaspoon sea salt

Directions:

1. Sit margarine out to soften.

2. Mix the dry ingredients in a small bowl and sit to the side.

3. In a large bowl, cream margarine by mixing with a hand mixer or spoon.

4. Add peanut butter and cream together with margarine. Then add sucanat and mix well.

5. Add vanilla and maple syrup and mix using hand mixer until smooth.

6. Add dry ingredients into wet a third at a time and mix with a spoon.

7. Cover in plastic wrap and let sit for at least 30 minutes.

8. Preheat oven to 350°F and lightly grease a cookie sheet or cover with parchment paper.

9. Using 1 tablespoon, scoop up dough and roll into balls. Place on cookie sheet and press down with fork. Repeat for all. [see above image]

10. Bake for 8-10 minutes, the bottoms should be golden brown.

Keep in mind that they continue to cook while on the pan. If they seem over cooked, bake for less time.

OATMEAL RAISIN COOKIES

YIELD 2 DOZEN
Soy Free, Gluten Free,
Dairy Free, Nut Free

Dry Ingredients:

1 cup all-purpose gluten free flour
1/2 teaspoon baking soda
1 tablespoon flax seed meal
1/2 teaspoon baking powder
1/2 teaspoon sea salt
1 teaspoon cinnamon
1/2 teaspoon ground cloves
1/2 teaspoon nutmeg
1 cup raisins
2 cups gluten free quick cooking oatmeal
1 cup chopped walnuts
      (optional)

Wet Ingredients:

1/3 cup non-dairy margarine
3/4 cup sucanat
1 tablespoon vanilla extract
1/2 cup maple syrup
2 tablespoon unsweetened non-dairy milk

Directions:

1. Sit margarine out to soften then in large bowl, cream margarine by mixing with a spoon.

2. Add sucanat and mix well.

3. Add vanilla, maple syrup and milk. Mix well.

4. In a separate bowl, mix the dry ingredients.

5. Add dry ingredients into wet a third at a time.

7. Cover with plastic wrap. Let sit for at least 30 minutes.

8. Preheat oven to 350°F and lightly grease a cookie sheet or use parchment paper.

9. Spoon dough onto sheet a heaping tablespoon at a time.

10. Bake for 10-12 minutes, the bottoms should be golden brown.

Keep in mind that they continue to cook while on the pan. If they seem over cooked, bake for less time.

CHEWY GRANOLA BARS

SERVES 8 PEOPLE

Soy Free, Gluten Free,
Dairy Free

Ingredients:

1 1/2 cups gluten free quick oats

1/3 cup finely shredded unsweetened coconut

1/2 tablespoon flax seed meal

1/3-1/2 cup chocolate chips

1/2 cup nuts or seeds roughly chopped
(peanuts, walnuts, pecans, pumpkin, or hemp)

Wet Ingredients:

1 cup coconut milk

1/3 cup unsweetened non-dairy milk

1/2 cup maple syrup

Directions:

1. Preheat oven to 375°F degrees. Then lightly oil an 8x8 pan.

2. In a small bowl, mix oats, coconut and flax meal. Set aside. In another bowl mix the wet ingredients.

4. Mix 1 cup of wet ingredients with the oat mix making sure it's all soaked. Then evenly spread the mix into the pan.

5. Top with nuts, then chocolate chips and pour the remaining liquid evenly over the nuts and chips.

6. Bake for 30 minutes until you hear sizzling. Edges should be lightly brown. Let cool the cut into 8 rectangular bars.

BOOGIE DOWN BROWNIES

MAKES 12 BROWNIES

Soy Free, Gluten Free, Dairy Free

Wet Ingredients:

1/2 teaspoon chia seeds +1/2 cup coconut milk

1/2 cup non dairy margarine or coconut oil

1 1/4 cup lightly sweetened chocolate chips

1/2 cup sucanat

1/4 cup maple syrup

1 tablespoon vanilla extract

Dry Ingredients:

1 1/4 cup all-purpose gluten free flour

1/2 teaspoon baking soda

1/2 teaspoon sea salt

1/2 teaspoon baking powder

2 tablespoon flax seed meal

1/2 cup chopped walnuts or pecans (optional)

Directions:

1. Pre heat oven to 350°F degrees. Then oil and flour a 9-inch square pan.

2. Mix chia seeds and coconut milk and sit to the side.

3. Heat a small pot on medium-low heat. Add the oil and chips. Mix until chips are melted. Add sucanat, maple syrup and vanilla and mix. Turn heat off.

4. Mix dry ingredients into a medium bowl. Using a whisk or hand mixer add chocolate and chia mixture into dry ingredients a little at a time making sure batter is well mixed.

5. Pour brownie batter into prepared pan and cook for 25 minutes.

6. They are done when a knife or toothpick are inserted and come out either clean or with light crumbs.

7. Let cool completely in the fridge before cutting.

SWEET POTATO PIE

SERVES 8 PEOPLE

Soy Free, Gluten Free,
Dairy Free, Nut Free

Ingredients:

3 cups of baked red garnet sweet potatoes
(about 4 medium)
1/4 cup agave
1/2 cup 100% maple syrup
3 tablespoons Ener-G egg replacer
1/2 tablespoon pure vanilla extract
1 teaspoon cinnamon
1 teaspoon nutmeg
1/4 teaspoon ground ginger
1/4 cup of melted non-dairy margarine

One 9" gluten free piecrust fresh or frozen
(see page 145)

Directions:

1. Bake unpeeled sweet potatoes in the oven at 450°F for 45-50 minutes, or until cooked all the way through.
2. Remove potatoes from oven and let cool enough to peel them.
3. Place an oven rack on 2nd to last shelf, then preheat the oven to 350°F.
4. Peel the potatoes then puree in a food processor.
5. Add egg replacer, agave, maple syrup, and vanilla to processor and mix well.
6. Heat cinnamon, nutmeg and ginger in a small skillet on medium-low heat for 30 seconds. Then add the margarine to the pan and melt.
7. Add the mixture to the potatoes and mix well.
8. Pour mixture into a piecrust then cover the rim of the piecrust with foil and place on bottom rack of the oven. (See below image)
9. Bake for 45-50 minutes where pie filling should be firm to touch.
10. Remove the foil during the last 10 minutes of baking to brown crust.

MANGO LASSI POPSICLES

MAKES 8-10 POPS

Soy Free, Gluten Free,
Dairy Free, Grain Free

Ingredients:

2 1/2 cups chopped mango, fresh or frozen (about 2 large mangoes)

1 1/2 cup coconut milk

1/4 cup agave

1/4 teaspoon ground cardamom

Directions:

1. Process all ingredients in a blender until smooth.

2. Transfer mixture to popsicle molds then add popsicle sticks and freeze until firm, 4-5 hours.

G-FREE PIECRUST

MAKES 2 CRUSTS

Soy Free, Gluten Free, Dairy Free, Nut Free

Ingredients:

2 cups all-purpose gluten free flour
1/4 teaspoon salt
1/2 cup non-dairy margarine, cut into cubes
1 tablespoon ENER-G egg replacer + 3 tablespoons water
2-3 tablespoons ice water
2 tablespoons agave or maple syrup
1 tablespoon vanilla extract

Directions:

1. Cut margarine into 1/2 inch pieces and place in the freezer for 15–30 minutes. In a small bowl mix egg replacer and water and sit to the side.

2. Combine the flour and salt in the bowl of a food processor or mixer. Pulse 5-6 times to combine. Add the margarine and pulse 6-8 times or until the mixture resembles coarse meal with some pea size pieces of margarine.

3. Mix together the egg replacer, water, agave and vanilla. With processor running, add the mixture until you get a slightly moist and sticky dough. Do not over mix. For gluten free dough its best to be too moist than too dry.

4. Remove the dough from the machine and form into 2 evenly sized disks. Wrap each disk in plastic wrap and let sit 15 minutes.

5. To roll the dough, lay a piece of waxed or parchment paper on a work surface and sprinkle paper, sprinkle with some more flour and lay on another piece of parchment paper. Roll the dough into a circle approximately 12 inches wide. You may have to remove the parchment paper on both sides and add a little more flour to make sure crust does not stick.

6. Remove top sheet of parchment paper and invert dough into pie/tart pan. Remove the top sheet of parchment paper and push the dough very gently down so it lines the bottom and sides of the pie plate. If the dough splits or breaks apart just push it back together. Trim the edge of the piecrust to about 1/2–3/4 inch over hang. Tuck the overhang under and pinch the dough into a decorative finish.

7. The other crust can either be used as a topping or can be refrigerated for up to 2 -3 days or put in freezer. Let sit out to warm slightly if in the fridge before use.

STRAWBERRY WAFFLE SHORTCAKE

SERVES 4 PEOPLE

Soy Free, Gluten Free,
Dairy Free

Waffles:

1 tablespoon flaxseed meal + 2 tablespoons non dairy milk

3/4 cup + 2 teaspoons non dairy milk + 2 teaspoons apple cider vinegar

3/4 cup +2 tablespoons all purpose gluten free flour

2 tablespoons cornstarch

1 teaspoon baking powder

3 tablespoons sucanat

1/4 teaspoon vanilla extract

1 tablespoon oil

Strawberry filling:

2 cups strawberries, halved or quartered depending on size

3 to 4 tablespoons agave or maple syrup

1 cup whipped cream (see page 39)

Directions:

For waffles

1. Add flaxseed meal to milk in a small bowl, mix well ad sit to the side.
2. Add apple cider vinegar to milk and sit to the side.
3. Mix together the flour, cornstarch, baking powder and sucanat into a large bowl.
4. Add flax mixture, vinegar mixture and remaining ingredients to the dry ingredients and mix well.
5. Let mixture sit for about five minutes and turn on waffle iron on high heat.
6. Lightly oil waffle iron and add 1 cup of waffle batter to iron. Close and cook until lightly brown. My waffle iron has a light that tells me when the waffle is done. I usually cook my waffle about 2-3 minutes longer until lightly golden brown.
7. Remove waffle and let cool on a wire rack to keep it crispy.
8. Repeat steps 6-7 for remaining waffles.

For strawberries:

1. Mix together the strawberries and agave and let sit for 10 minutes.

Assemble:

1. Separate waffle into 4 pieces.
2. Top 1 waffle piece with about 2 tablespoons of strawberry mixture and 1-2 tablespoons whipped cream.
3. Top with another waffle and about 2 tablespoons of strawberry mixture and 1-2 tablespoons whipped cream.

5 SPICE RICE CRISPY TREATS

SERVES 12 PEOPLE

Gluten Free, Dairy Free,
Nut Free

Ingredients:

4 tablespoons non dairy margarine

4 cups vegan marshmallows

1/4 teaspoon 5 spice powder

4 cups crispy brown rice cereal

Directions:

1. Oil a 9x13-inch baking dish (or a smaller dish — see Note below).

2. In a heavy saucepan melt margarine over medium-low heat. Fold in the marshmallows and 5 spice, stirring frequently until almost completely melted.

3. Add the puffed rice cereal and stir until combined.

4. Press the mixture into the greased rectangular baking dish. Let set for 30 minutes before cutting and serving.

**Note: I call for a 9x13-inch dish here, but I often use an 8x11-inch because I like taller treats. Any size in this range should do.

JUICY FRUIT CRUMBLE

SERVES 4-6 PEOPLE

Soy Free, Gluten Free,
Dairy Free, Nut Free

Filling:

5-6 cups of fruit, chopped*

1 teaspoon cinnamon

1/2 teaspoon nutmeg

1/2 cup maple syrup

1/4 cup coconut sugar

Juice of 1/2 lemon

1 tablespoon cornstarch (or arrowroot) + 1 tablespoon non-dairy milk.

Topping:

1 cup gluten free rolled oats

1/4 cup all purpose gluten free flour

1 tablespoon flax seed meal

2 tablespoons coconut sugar

1/4 cup non-dairy margarine or oil

2 tablespoons non-dairy milk

Directions:

1. Pre heat oven to 350 degrees and lightly oil an 8x8 pan.

2. Add all filling ingredients except cornstarch to a small pot. Cover and simmer on medium low heat for 5 minutes.

3. While fruit is cooking, mix together the oats, flour, flax seed and coconut sugar in a small bowl.

4. Add margarine and mix together with dry mixture until mixed well (use your hands if necessary).

5. Add milk and mix well.

6. Mix together cornstarch and milk in a small cup then add to fruit mixture.

7. Pour fruit mixture into pan then spoon over the dry mixture, lightly spreading it across the fruit.

8. Put pan on a baking sheet and bake for 20-25 minutes.

**Note: A range of fruits can be used. Use just one fruit or a mix of a few. Spring fruits: berries and figs; Summer fruits- plums, peaches, and nectarines; Fall fruits: apple and pear.

SMASHING PUMPKIN MUFFINS

MAKES 12 LARGE MUFFINS OR 16 SMALL

Soy Free, Gluten Free, Dairy Free, Nut Free

Dry Ingredients:

2 cups all-purpose gluten free flour

2 teaspoons baking powder

2 tablespoons flax seed meal

1 teaspoon cinnamon

1/2 teaspoon nutmeg

1/4 teaspoon cloves

1/4 teaspoon sea salt

1/2 cup pumpkin seeds (optional)

Wet Ingredients:

1/2 cup unsweetened non dairy milk + 1/8 tsp chia seeds

3/4 cup non dairy margarine (at room temp)

3/4 cup maple syrup

1 cup coconut sugar

1/2 teaspoon vanilla

1/2 teaspoon fresh grated ginger

1 teaspoon molasses

1 can mashed pumpkin

Directions:

Preheat oven to 400˚.

1. Use muffin cups or oil and flour a 12-muffin pan. Set aside.

2. Add chia seeds to milk and set to the side.

3. In a large bowl mix the dry ingredients.

4. In a separate bowl, cream margarine using a hand mixer, then add coconut sugar and mix well.

5. Add the remaining wet ingredients and mix well.

6. Add wet ingredients to dry a third at a time and mix well.

7. Pour batter into muffin pan

8. Bake for 20-25 minutes until toothpick poked in comes out clean.

ICE CREAM BURGERS

MAKES 8 BURGERS

Soy Free, Gluten Free,
Dairy Free, Nut Free

Wet Ingredients:

2 teaspoons vanilla

1/4 cup maple syrup

1/2 cup sucanat

1/3 cup vegan margarine

1 pint of your favorite non-dairy ice cream

Dry Ingredients:

1 cup +2 tablespoons all purpose gluten free flour

1/2 teaspoon baking soda

1/2 teaspoon baking powder

1 tablespoon flax seed meal

5 teaspoons carob or cocoa powder (optional)**

Directions:

1. Sit margarine out to soften.

2. In a large bowl, cream margarine by mixing with a spoon.

3. Add sucanat and mix well.

4. Add vanilla and maple syrup. Mix well.

5. In a separate bowl, mix the dry ingredients.

6. Add dry ingredients into wet a third at a time.

7. Cover and refrigerate for at least 30 minutes.

8. Preheat oven to 350° and lightly grease a cookie sheet or cover with parchment paper.

9. Spoon dough onto sheet 1 tablespoon at a time.

10. Bake for 10-12 minutes. (The bottoms should be golden brown)

11. Keep in mind that they continue to cook while on pan. If they seem over cooked, bake for less time.

12. Let cookies cool completely. While cookies are cooling sit out ice cream to soften.

13. Scoop 2 tablespoons of ice cream onto 1 cookie. Sit on a flat surface and evenly spread ice cream on cookie. Top with another cookie and place into a freezer friendly container.

14. Repeat step 13 until all cookies are used. Cover container and freeze cookies for 3-4 hours.

** Adding carob or cocoa powder will make chocolate cookies as opposed to vanilla. Adding the powder will make the cookies slightly thicker.

GEORGIA PEACH PIE

MAKES ONE 9" PIE

Soy Free, Gluten Free,
Dairy Free, Nut Free

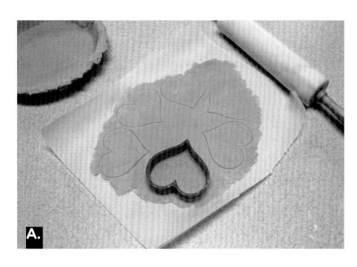

A.

Ingredients:

2 gluten free piecrusts frozen or fresh (see page 145)
4-4 1/2 cups of peaches fresh or frozen
1/4 cup non-dairy margarine
1/4 cup unsweetened non-dairy milk
1/2 teaspoon vanilla extract
3/4 cup maple syrup
1/4 teaspoon nutmeg
1/4 teaspoon cinnamon
Pinch of salt
1 tablespoon + 1 teaspoon arrowroot or cornstarch +3 tablespoons unsweetened non-dairy milk

Directions:

1. Preheat oven to 350°F degrees and place an oven rack on the last shelf.
2. Cut peaches into small chunks. Add to a medium pot, cover and simmer on medium-low heat for 10 minutes if frozen. If using fresh cook for 5 minutes.
3. Add remaining ingredients except arrowroot or cornstarch to peaches. Cover and simmer on a medium-low heat for 5 minutes. Turn off.
4. In a small cup, mix arrowroot or cornstarch and milk then add to peach mixture.
5. Pour peach mixture in one of the piecrusts and reserve 3 tablespoons of liquid.
6. If using a frozen crust let the second one defrost lightly. Place the second crust on top and use a fork to close OR use a cookie cutter to cut out hearts and layer around pie. (see above image)
7. Brush all of the reserved liquid on to crust.
8. Sit pie on cookie sheet to prevent dripping. Bake on last shelf of oven for 20-25 minutes.
9. Serve warm topped with your favorite nondairy vanilla ice cream.

Sorrel Sizzurp
(pg 160)

left to right:
**Chlorophyll
Lemonade (pg 158);
Matcha (pg 161)**

clockwise eft to right:
Bitches Brew (pg 162);
Sweet Chilli Sauce (pg 166);
Mango Salsa (pg 163)

POUR UP...DRANK
BEVERAGES

chlorophyll lemonade

red velvet lemonade

pineapple green tea

sorrel sizzurp

green lantern smoothie

matcha

bitches brew

THE VEGAN REMIX
SAUCE IT UP
TASTY TOUCHES

mango salsa

bbq sauce

"honey" mustard dressing

berbere - ethiopian spice mix

sweet chilli sauce

CHLOROPHYLL LEMONADE

SERVES 8-10 PEOPLE

Soy Free, Gluten Free,
Dairy Free, Nut Free, Grain Free

Ingredients:

2 teaspoons of liquid chlorophyll or 12-15 drops of chlorophyll concentrate

12 cups water, divided

Juice of 2 lemons

1/2 cup agave or to taste

Directions:

1. Juice the lemons into a large pitcher.

2. Add agave, 2 cups of water and chlorophyll and mix well.

3. Add remaining water and mix

RED VELVET LEMONADE

SERVES 8 PEOPLE

Soy Free, Gluten Free,
Dairy Free, Nut Free, Grain Free

Ingredients:

1/2 cup frozen cherries or strawberries

1¼ cup lemon juice (about 7 lemons)**

1½ cup agave

7 cups water, divided

**Pre made lemon juice works just as well.

Directions:

1. Blend the cherries and 1 cup of water in a blender.

2. Juice the lemons and add to a small pitcher along with the agave. Mix well then add remaining ingredients.

3. Serve chilled.

PINEAPPLE GREEN TEA

SERVES 8- 10 PEOPLE

Soy Free, Gluten Free,
Dairy Free, Nut Free, Grain Free

Ingredients:

7 green tea bags
12 cups of hot water
3/4-1 cup agave
2 cups frozen or fresh pineapples, divided**

Directions:

1. Boil water in a kettle or pot then add to a glass pitcher.

2. Add 3/4 cup of agave and mix well. Next add tea bags and let steep for 10 minutes.

3. Put 1 cup of tea and 1/2 cup of pineapples in a blender and mix well. Add to pitcher.

4. Then add remaining pineapples to pitcher. Let sit for 30 minutes.

5. Taste to see if it's sweet enough for you. If not, add remaining agave and mix well.

Mangos can also be used

SORREL SIZZURP

SERVES 8-10 PEOPLE
Soy Free, Gluten Free, Dairy Free,
Nut Free, Grain Free

Ingredients:

12 cups water

2 cups dried sorrel **

1 cup agave or to taste

2 inches of ginger, cut in 4 slices

1 stick of cinnamon

1/2 teaspoon ground allspice

4 whole cloves

Directions:

1. Bring water to a boil in a medium pot then add all ingredients and turn off heat.
2. Cover and let steep for a minimum of 4 hours to overnight. If steeping overnight put in the refrigerator.
3. Strain and taste. If you want it sweeter add 1/4 - 1/2 cup more agave.
4. Serve cold.

** **If you cannot find Sorrel, Hibiscus can be used as a substitute.**

GREEN LANTERN SMOOTHIE

**MAKES TWO
10 OZ SERVINGS**

Soy Free, Gluten Free,
Dairy Free, Nut Free, Grain Free

Ingredients:

1 frozen banana

1/2 cup frozen pineapple

2 cups spinach

1/4 cup pumpkin seeds

1 cup unsweetened non-dairy milk

1 tablespoon agave (optional)

A couple of ice cubes (optional)

Directions:

Add all ingredients into a blender and mix well.

MATCHA

SERVES 3 PEOPLE

Soy Free, Gluten Free,
Dairy Free, Nut Free, Grain Free

Ingredients:

1 teaspoon green tea powder (matcha)

1/4 cup warm water (but not boiling)

3 tablespoons agave or to taste

1 1/2 cup unsweetened non dairy milk

1 teaspoon vanilla extract

2-3 cups ice cubes

Directions:

1. In a small bowl, mix green tea powder in water.
2. Stir with a whisk until completely dissolved. Then stir in agave.
3. Add milk and remaining ingredients to blender. And blend until smooth

BITCHES BREW

SERVES 2-4 PEOPLE

Soy Free, Gluten Free,
Dairy Free, Nut Free, Grain Free

Ingredients:

4 peppermint tea bags

2 cups boiling water

2 cups non-dairy milk

3 teaspoons carob powder **

5 1/2 teaspoons agave

Directions:

1. Bring water to a boil in a medium pot. Turn off; add tea bags, cover and let sit for 10 minutes.

2. In a small cup mix carob powder with 2 tablespoons of the water from the tea. Mix well and sit to the side.

3. Add milk and agave to tea mixture, then heat on medium heat just enough to warm but not boil.

4. Add the carob mixture, remove tea bags and serve.

** **Unsweetened cocoa powder can be substituted for carob powder**

MANGO SALSA

SERVES 4 PEOPLE

Soy Free, Gluten Free,
Dairy Free, Nut Free, Grain Free

Ingredients:

1 ripe mango, peeled, pitted, and diced
(about 1½ cups)
1/2 cup medium red onion, finely chopped
1 tablespoon Jalapeño pepper, minced
(remove the seeds if you want it mild)
2 cups tomatoes, chopped small
3 tablespoons fresh cilantro leaves, minced
1 teaspoon minced jalapeño,
seeded (optional)
3 tablespoons fresh lime juice
1/4 teaspoon sea salt or to taste

Directions:

Combine all of the ingredients in a bowl. Let sit
for a minimum of 5 minutes.

BBQ SAUCE

SERVES 6-8 PEOPLE

Soy Free, Gluten Free,
Dairy Free, Nut Free, Grain Free

Ingredients:

1/2 cup ketchup

1 tablespoon molasses

2 teaspoon granulated garlic or garlic powder

1 teaspoon chili powder

1 teaspoon salt

1 teaspoon black pepper

1/2 teaspoon smoked paprika

1/2 cup water

Directions:

Add sauce ingredients to a small pot and simmer for 20 minutes stirring occasionally.

"HONEY" MUSTARD DRESSING

MAKES ABOUT 1/3 CUP

Soy Free, Gluten Free,
Dairy Free, Nut Free, Grain Free

Ingredients:

3 tablespoons mustard

3 tablespoons + 1 teaspoon agave

1/4 teaspoon sea salt

2 tablespoons olive or sesame oil

Pinch red pepper flakes

Directions:

Mix dressing ingredients in a small bowl and use as a dressing or dip.

BERBERE
(ETHIOPIAN SPICE MIX)

MAKES ABOUT 2/3 CUP

Soy Free, Gluten Free,
Dairy Free, Nut Free, Grain Free

Ingredients:

1/2 teaspoon ground allspice

3 teaspoons ground cardamom

1/4 teaspoon ground cinnamon

1/4 teaspoon ground cloves

1 teaspoon ground coriander

1 teaspoon ground cumin

1 teaspoon ground fenugreek

1 teaspoon ground black pepper

1/2 teaspoon ground turmeric

6 tablespoons paprika

1 teaspoon granulated garlic or garlic powder

2 teaspoons sea salt

2 teaspoons ground ginger

1/2 -1 teaspoon cayenne depending on how hot you like it

Directions:

Mix all ingredients and place in a tightly covered container.
This mixture can be used with many combinations of legumes, rice or vegetables

SWEET CHILI SAUCE

MAKES 1/3 CUP

Soy Free, Gluten Free,
Dairy Free, Nut Free

Ingredients:

1/4 cup water

1 tablespoon toasted sesame oil

3 teaspoons agave

1 teaspoon mirin

1-1 1/2 teaspoon fresh Thai chilies, minced

2 teaspoon minced garlic

2 tablespoons fresh lime or lemon juice

1/4 teaspoon cornstarch + 1/4 teaspoon water

1/4 teaspoon salt

Directions:

1. Combine all ingredients in a medium saucepan except cornstarch and water, then bring the sauce to a boil.

2. As the sauce is coming to a boil, make the cornstarch slurry by combining the cornstarch and water in a small bowl. Make sure to stir the slurry well and break up any lumps of cornstarch.

3. When the sauce comes to a boil, gently stir in the cornstarch slurry. Slowly stir the sauce till it thickens. Once the sauce thickens, turn off heat. Allow to cool.

4. It's easy to double recipe if you want and keeps up to 7 days in refrigerator

ABOUT THE AUTHOR

Afya Ibomu is a Holistic Nutritionist, the CEO of NATTRAL.com, and has been plant based since 1990. Her third book *The Vegan Soul Food Guide to the Galaxy*, was nominated for an African American Literary Award for cookbook of the year.

Afya is certified in Holistic Health and holds a bachelor's degree in nutrition. She is also the author of the *Get Your Crochet On!* pattern book series, that have sold over 25,000 copies. Afya is a celebrity nutritionist and crochet designer working with hip hop artists such as Erykah Badu, Common, Dead Prez and Talib Kweli.

Afya currently conducts cooking demos and classes, teaches nutrition workshops and counsels fitness competitors. She lives in Atlanta with her husband stic of dead prez and their son Itwela.

To keep up with what afya is doing, check her out on all social media platforms @afyaibomu.

Other books by this author:
Get Your Crochet On! Hip Hats and Cool Caps
Get Your Crochet On! Fly Tops and Funky Flavas
The Vegan Soul Food Guide to the Galaxy
Eat Plants, Lift Iron (co author)

INDEX